THE BEAR, THE BULL AND THE BUTTERFLY

A Journey To Authentic Healing

BY
Mary-Joy Albutt

ISBN (PB): 979-8-89604-087-3

ISBN (HB): 979-8-89604-088-0

Table of Contents

Dedication

This book is dedicated to Amanda, who has held everything that I have shared in that sacred space between counsellor and counselee with love, understanding, and compassion. You have journeyed with me to places of unimaginable horror, helped me rescue the fragmented pieces, and gently encouraged me to rewrite a new ending to my story.

And to Peter, my rock, my soul mate, my protector, my defender. You have always believed me and believed *in* me, and taught me what it means to love and be loved.

About the Author

Mary-Joy (known as "M-J") lives in the Midlands (UK) with her husband and two sausage dogs!

Since qualifying as a nurse (Registered General Nurse and Registered Mental Nurse) in 1989 she has had a varied career in nursing, further education and public health. This includes specialising in HIV nursing in 1998 and then spending 4 years travelling across India as an HIV educator.

More recently, she has specialised in dementia care and is currently working as Head of Dementia for a large private healthcare company. In her spare time, she is studying for a PhD, researching the links between trauma and dementia and how healthcare staff can provide trauma informed dementia care within nursing / care home settings.

She likes to be physically active and loves to be outdoors. She took up running at the age of 55 and has run a number of half marathons to raise money for dementia charities. Her latest adventure is to trek across the Sahara to raise money for the Alzheimer's society.

If you would like to contact Mary-Joy, you can do so via her website: www.aimtogetbetter.com

Acknowledgment

I am so grateful to the small group of people who make up my new "tribe". Breaking away from historical, toxic relationships has been made so much easier because, in the process, I have discovered true friends who allow me to be my authentic self.

I would also like to thank Diane Bushell, my “critical friend” who gave so many supportive suggestions after reading my original manuscript.

Most of all, I would like to thank Peter Albutt, my husband of almost 20 years. He gets hardly any mentions in this book, mainly because I do not have the words to describe what he means to me or how very grateful I am that he found me, rescued me, believed me, supported me and never gave up on me. He speaks very little about how it was for him when I sank to the depths, or the loneliness he felt whilst he patiently waited for me to resurface. I have no doubt that I would not still be here if it wasn't for him.

Introduction

In the last ten to fifteen years, mental health professionals and the general population have become increasingly aware of the lifelong effects that traumatic experiences can have on an individual. With this increased awareness has come more understanding about the process of "triggering", where an event in the here and now can trigger a person to experience flashbacks, re-experiencing a memory which may have occurred decades ago, as if it is happening in the present. During this process, a person may also experience dissociation.

I am not going to attempt to explain the effects of trauma or the mechanisms of dissociation in this book—numerous authors have already written about them in a far more cohesive way than I could ever do (see references and recommended reading on p. 214 for the ones I have found most helpful).

What I *am* going to do is describe what it feels like to be *living with* those effects on a daily basis and the challenges I have faced on the journey towards healing.

In my early twenties, instead of feeling like an adult, I felt like I had a whole family of out-of-control children inside of me, and I had no idea, from moment to moment, which of them would be in control of my emotions and behaviours. No one seemed to understand. Even during my many admissions to psychiatric hospitals, which started at the age of 16, I felt that the staff judged me, and I was given many negative labels, such as "time-wasting", "attention-seeking", and "personality-disorder".

In the early 1990s, a psychologist told me about the process of dissociation. Although this may have explained *why* I felt like I had all of these fragmented child parts inside of me, it didn't stop them from running riot, and it did not stop the cycles of behaviours that would continue for the next twenty-five years.

At the age of 24, I became more aware of these children inside of me and I started to have vivid flashbacks of childhood sexual abuse. I began discovering memories each of which linked to each child inside me.

As I started to disclose these memories, some people wanted to believe me, but my father was a Baptist minister, respected as a spirit-filled Christian man. This made it almost impossible for those in the church to believe he was capable of doing such things. My story did not make sense in the light of the "all or nothing" Christian faith; you were either a Christian, born-again, filled with the Holy Spirit and going to heaven, or you were not born-again, filled with darkness and going to hell. There was nothing in between. It was impossible that such a godly, born-again, spiritual man could do such evil things. Instead of questioning their own doctrines, people questioned what I was saying and decided not to believe my story.

One of my brothers, who at the time was an elder in the church I went to, convinced both me and the people trying to support me that, although what was going on in my head was very real to me, an evil spirit of deception was causing my “memories”. Over the next 10 years, until I left the church and lost my Christian beliefs completely, I had many experiences, in a variety of different Christian settings, of people trying to cast evil spirits out of me, either to take the memories away or to stop my dysfunctional and self-harming behaviours. It didn’t work.

During a hospital admission in 2001, another brother, a doctor at the Department of Health, visited me regularly. After a meeting between my consultant and my brother, it was decided that the memories were due to psychosis. I was prescribed antipsychotics for the next 20+ years.

But the memories have never gone away. There have been periods when I was able to convince myself I was making them up or that I was psychotic, but whatever I did, and however hard I tried to block them out, the memories still kept resurfacing.

In 2012, I finally identified what my triggers were, so I actively avoided them. Consequently, I had almost ten years of staying "well" and, to some extent, experiencing joy in life. But in 2021, it all "went wrong" again, and I was back in crisis.

But this time, everything had changed. Mental health services had become "trauma-informed". Instead of experiencing intolerance, judgement, and labelling from the professionals I spoke to, I felt understood. People empathetically explained why I felt the way I did and why I wanted to behave the way I did and taught me alternative ways of dealing with the extreme feelings that overwhelmed me when I was experiencing flashbacks. But, most of all, I felt *believed.*

I started seeing a counsellor in November 2021 and started on the journey towards authentic healing. It had taken me until I was 55 to get to the starting line.

I hope that, by reading my story, others will realise that it is never too late to embark on the journey towards authentic healing.

This book is presented in five parts:

Part I – Introducing the Children Inside

Part I of this book introduces the children inside me and their experiences, allowing their stories to be told and their voices to be heard for the first time.

It also gives an insight into living as an adult with a trauma-related dissociative disorder.

Trigger Warning: If you have experienced childhood abuse or sexual abuse as an adult, it is possible that you could be triggered by reading Part I. If there is a possibility that you could be affected in this way, before reading, please consider taking the following steps:

1) *Go straight to Parts III, IV, and V, which focus on the healing process and the hope of transformation.*
2) *Make sure you are in a safe (not public) place and that you are not alone when reading this book.*

3) *Make sure you have someone to talk to or have access to a helpline in case you need to talk about the feelings that have come up for you.*

4) *Before reading Part I, go to www.aimtogetbetter.com/ or scan the QR code, where you will find tips on making yourself an emergency first-aid box and exercises on returning to the present when you have been triggered.*

5) *On the title page of Part I and at the end of the book, on the last page, there will be a QR code to immediately take you to the above webpage. Please ensure you use this as soon as you feel the first signs that you are being triggered – do not allow your feelings to escalate to the point of you becoming overwhelmed.*

Part II – The Bear

This section introduces us to the Bear – the elaborate disguises and defensive cages we learn to live behind, the complex psychological mechanisms and behaviours that our brain employs as a desperate survival strategy when our existence is persistently under threat. It goes on to explore why, in order to experience authentic healing, we have to go through a process of taking down the defences, shedding the layers and letting go of the dysfunctional, defensive, self-protective feelings and behaviours we use to survive.

Part III – The Bull

We move on to recognise the Bull, who symbolises all the disabling and deceptive thought processes we have developed over time through the brainwashing, gaslighting, manipulation and lies employed by the persistent abuser to keep us in a permanent submissive state. It demonstrates how the process of "changing our mind" can be painfully slow and requires patience, determination and tenacity.

Part IV – The Journey

This section explains why I am on this journey and what keeps me going, even when it seems I spend more time sitting in the bottom of pits and going around in circles rather than going forward. It gives insight into why it is so important that we take our own path; if we simply follow the paths of others, we may never find our true destiny. If we have been forced and coerced onto a different path by the actions of others, it is never too late to turn around and divert back to where we should have always been.

Part V – The Songs of the Butterfly

This section, full of hope and the joy of transformation, celebrates the experience of finding my true destiny and emerging into my full potential. When I am in my darkest places of despair, instead of resorting to the old behaviours, I have learnt to be still and listen for the "Song of the Butterfly".

The book contains numerous references to my Christian upbringing and former beliefs about God. I considered whether I should leave them out, because I was concerned that it may make the book inaccessible to those who do not hold such beliefs. But I couldn't. Partly because there would not be much content left but also because, by leaving them in, I hope to demonstrate how living in a highly religious environment for the first 40 years of my life added layers of complexity to my story, making the process of "de-programming" and disentangling the truth of who I am from all the lies and deception even more difficult and long-winded than it may otherwise have been. Many of the poems in parts IV and V will demonstrate that I have moved on to a different type of spirituality. For those who have no religious beliefs and do not practice any form of spirituality, I hope you can still gain something from the hope and healing that is evident in my writing.

Prologue

Can you hear my silent screams?

Can you hear my silent screams?
Echoing through the night?
Can you hear the cries of pain
I'm shouting with all my might.

Please come a bit closer, and you will see
That things really aren't how they seem;
Please listen harder to the unspoken words
And hear stories that should never have been.

Please, come and touch so you can feel
The trauma and the pain
Dive down into these murky depths -
So deep you may never resurface again.

This is my world, the one that's been
Hidden for many years.
This is my hurt, my anguish, my pain;
These are my bottled-up tears.

If only there was someone who could enter my world,
Who could experience this hell with me;
If only they could come into those dark, scary nights,
Help me fight and cut myself free.

Come, search with me, and you will find a girl of three
Locked up behind closed doors;
Dig deep and behind the thick, hard walls
You'll find, abandoned, a child of four.

Keep looking, keep searching, and you will find
Many children crying out in pain.
If you stop to find out what they've been through
You'll discover a sick and frightening game.

They've all had their love and trust abused,
They've all been badly hurt,
They all think they've done something terribly wrong,
They all feel filled with dirt.

They feel that it must have been their fault,
That somehow, they are to blame.
They all think that they should have tried to fight more,
To stop it happening again.

They think that something must be wrong with them
That really, it's them that's bad;
They should have said 'no' and stopped what went on -
They deserve to be punished and feel sad.

So now they're tormented and extremely disturbed,
They want to express their pain.
They want to get rid of the hurt and the dirt;
They want to feel clean again...

Can you hear my silent screams?
Echoing through your ears?
Can you discover those children in pain?
Feel the hurt they've felt for years?

Please— come closer—don't walk away,
Don't try to turn a blind eye;
Those children are trying their best to be heard;
If not, they will probably die.

The children want love; they want to feel someone cares,
They want to be understood;
They want to express the way they feel
So they can grow up the way all children should.

Although these children have their own stories to tell,
They are all different parts of me;
They need to be seen, heard and understood,
To be let out, so I can be free.

Can you hear my silent screams?
Echoing through the night...

MJA, 14.5.93

PART I

Introducing the Children Inside

Chapter 1

The Day My Life Was Changed Forever – Introducing My Three-Year-Old.

It should have been a lovely day at the seaside. A day of making memories in the summer sunshine. At the age of three, I was confident in the water and loved splashing around.

We didn't live near the sea, so when we were on holiday, we used to plead with our parents to "take us out deep" so we could practice treading water and swimming.

When my father agreed to "take me out deep," I entered the water excited and feeling special because I didn't often get his one-to-one attention.

He was supporting me under my arms while I kicked frantically to keep my head above the waves. And then it happened…

One of his hands moved from under my arms to between my legs.

I did not know what he was doing, but I knew I didn't like it.

As a Baptist minister, the one aspect of my father's job that he enjoyed the most, the thing that gave him a sense of purpose more than anything else, was taking new converts to the Christian faith through the ritual of baptism. This is where the minister stands in a pool of water with the new convert, then tips them backwards so they are completely immersed in the water, and then he pulls them out again. This ritual symbolises the washing away of the person's sins. They enter the water defiled by their sin but emerge cleansed and purified and, therefore, able to move forward in a guilt-free relationship with their God.

I have never, ever been able to get my head around the irony. I cannot make any sense of it. That the man who seemed to live for the moment when he could take people into those waters to cleanse them from their sin took his own daughter into the waters and changed her forever, in the completely opposite way.

She went into the water that day as an excited, innocent three-year-old, happy to be on holiday, feeling special because she had been chosen rather than her brothers to "go out deep" with her dad.

But she emerged from that water defiled and confused, weighed down by a sense of guilt that should not have been hers to carry.

Her relationship with her father, her body and her inner self had changed in an instant.

From that moment on, she would never be able to be in close proximity to him without feeling tainted, filthy, polluted, ashamed and smeared with slime. Every time he came near her, she wanted to vomit, as if he were surrounded by a noxious, nauseating cloud that only she could smell.

Chapter 2

The Teddies And The Wallpaper – Introducing My Three-And-A-Half-Year-Old

A few months later, I am in my bedroom. I find a compass, and with all my might, I use it to scratch out all the teddy bears from the wallpaper.

My mum comes in and gets very cross, shouting, “What are you doing?” She is terribly upset that I have defaced the beautiful wallpaper.

I try to explain.

The teddies are not teddies. They are monsters that come out of the wallpaper at night and do terrible things to me in the dark. She tells me not to be so silly…

My brothers come into the room to see why my mum was shouting. I am now crying, desperately trying to make them all understand that I am terrified, that the teddies are awful monsters that come to life in the dark. They all laugh at me, telling me there is no such things as monsters.

I am in a panic. I need them to believe me. Why won't they listen?

My father comes into the room. Mum shows him the wall. My brother tells him mockingly that I believe monsters are coming into my room at night. My father shouts, tells me I am a very naughty girl for damaging the wallpaper, tells me off for telling lies and smacks me.

Instead of protecting me and reassuring me, they mocked me, told me off for making things up and punished me. No one believed me when I desperately needed them to.

I am left to face the monsters alone.

I am terrified.

The spark of hope that someone would rescue me is extinguished as something deep inside of me dies.

The Teddies in the Wallpaper

A thousand knives are twisting in my heart,
I cannot describe the pain;
I dare not breathe, I cannot move,
In case they come again.

I cannot explain the turmoil inside.
Or my fear as I lie in my bed;
I cannot cope with the confusion I feel -
It would be better if I could be dead.

What was that shadow? How could it do such a thing?
Was it the teddies and frogs in the wall?
It seemed like my daddy, that was hurting me so,
But my daddy's not like that at all.

My daddy's a nice man; my daddy's not bad:
It must have been the teddies that got into my bed!
But how would I cope if they came out to play again?
To make sure they can't hurt me, I have to make myself dead.

I'll pretend my insides are not alive,
I'll forget and bury the pain;
Although on the outside, my body may grow,
Inside, I'll die, so I can't be hurt again...

So, on that night in '69.
A three-year-old was killed.
No one can imagine the torture involved,
But at least her pain was stilled.

Nobody noticed the murder take place;
As trauma ripped her apart like a knife.
But after all these years, a strange thing is happening;
She is coming back to life...

The memories, the pain, the fear, and the despair,
The confusion and the broken heart,
The disgust, the disdain, and the desire to die
Are as strong as they were at the start.

I can't get away; I can get no release,
I keep losing hope of finding any peace.
I don't know how to cope or how to deal with the pain,
Unless the child dies again.

For months, I have fought and fought to survive,
In the hope that I could get free,
But it seems that in order to ease the pain,
I have to do away with me

I wish there was some way for the children inside me
To grow up and be part of me;
I wish they'd stop hurting so I could behave
Like the adult I really should be.

I keep trying to move forward and pretend they're not there;
I just want to get on with my life,
But the more I ignore them and push them away
The more I end up in strife.

So, although on the outside I seem grown up,
On the inside are many children in pain.
They all want to be accepted and understood -
To go back and be mothered again.

I wish there was someone who could see what was done,
Who could go back with them through the years;
Someone to be there on those dark, scary nights,
Who understands their fears.

But because I know it can't be done,
I am filled with pain and despair;
I don't want those young girls to be part of me
I'd do anything for them not to be there.

So, the only answer is for me to die;
Make sure all the children are killed.
It's the only way to end their torture and grief
And for their torment to be stilled.

I'm sorry if I hurt the people who care,
But I hope you understand?
Inside of me are children who are really scared
But have no one to hold their hand.

It's better for them if I let them die,
Than to be stuck in that terrible past;
It's better for me to say goodbye,
So that they can be free at last.

MJA, May 1995

Chapter 3

The Lamb To The Slaughter –Introducing The Four-Year-Old Me

"Jesus tender shepherd, hear me,
Bless thy little lamb tonight,
Through the darkness be thou near me,
Keep me safe 'til morning light."
Amen

Every night, when my mum came to settle me into bed, she prayed a prayer, and then we sang this song. I even had a little plaque on my bedroom wall, above the bookcase, with the words of the song on it.

I sang that song with all my might every night. God only knows how sincerely I sang those words and how desperate I was for Him to answer them.

But a few hours later…

I can't breathe, there is such a tightness round my neck. There is a weight on top of me, so heavy, it is crushing me. I am consumed with panic. I want to push the weight off me, but it is so heavy I can't move. I try to scream, but every time I try to make a sound the tightness round my neck means that I cannot breathe, and it feels like my head is going to explode.

I open my eyes just a tiny bit – in the darkness there is the outline of big, black silhouette looming over me........

The monster is back.

I squeeze my eyes tight shut again. The fear, the panic, the terror, the tightness round my throat is too much for my little body and soul to bear. Somehow, from somewhere deep inside, I find a switch to turn the nightmare off. Like turning off a horror movie on the TV, I dive down to a place very, very deep inside myself to escape the sensations in my body and the terror in my soul..........

......I am curled up in a tight ball, hiding under the covers. My head is pounding so hard that I think the blood is going to burst through my ears and my eyes. I feel sick. I can hardly breathe because I am trying so hard to make sure I don't let out any of the sobs and the silent screams that are choking me. If I start to let them out, they will be so loud, the entire world will be woken up by them.

But far worse than any of the sensations in my body is the sense of overwhelming darkness inside of me. The song I sang to Jesus is ringing in my ears... "through the darkness be thou near me, keep me safe 'til morning light."

"Where were you Jesus? I sang my song with all my might. I sang it the best I could. I prayed with my whole heart that you would be near me and keep me safe. Why didn't you listen? Why did the monster come back? Why didn't anyone stop him? Why didn't you rescue me? Why didn't anyone rescue me?"

Although I know the monster has gone and the teddies have gone back into the wallpaper, somehow the heavy weight that was lying on top of me is now inside of me.

The darkness inside me is far darker than the room around me. I am drowning on the inside, my little spirit submerged in dirt.

MJA Nov 2021

Chapter 4

The Monster Daddy – Introducing The Five-Year-Old Me

I am petrified of the dark. For some time now, I have had to sleep with my bedroom door ajar and the landing light on. Every time my mum settles me to sleep, the last thing I say to her is, "Can you leave the landing light on?"

If the light is not on, I will lie in bed and shout until someone hears me.

I wake up in pitch-black darkness. I am about to start shouting when I realise there is a large shadow. The monster is sitting on the edge of my bed. I freeze.

Suddenly, the landing light turns on. I see my mum at the doorway to my room. I am filled with relief – she has saved me from the monster. "Is everything alright?"

But instead of the monster replying, I hear my father's voice, "She's fine. She has just had a bad dream. I will stay with her until she goes back to sleep." With this, she goes to the toilet and then returns to her room, turning off the landing light. At the same time, a light goes out inside my soul—a glimmer of hope that I was going to be rescued from the monster is extinguished, and a weight of hopelessness replaces it.

He reaches over my body and puts a strong hand on my arm, so I can't move it. He puts his other hand on my belly and starts rubbing it in circular motions. "You're OK, Daddy's here. Daddy loves you, and you're his special little girl, aren't you?" He repositions himself, so he is on top of me. I can't breathe. I cannot move. I am squashed. I am petrified. But I can still hear his voice, "Daddy loves you. You're Daddy's special girl, but you must not tell anyone; if you do, they will say you are bad and send you away. This is our special secret."

And then, a realisation hits my 5-year-old brain that I find impossible to process:

It wasn't a monster doing all these terrible things to me, and it wasn't the teddy bears coming out of the wallpaper.

It would have been so much easier if I could have continued believing that it was.

There is a verse in the Bible that says, "You will know the truth, and the truth will set you free."

This truth did not set me free. It imprisoned me in a dark, secret world of conflict and confusion that I would be trapped inside of for the next 50 years.

My Two Daddies

I just don't understand something about my daddy. It seems like he isn't one daddy but two different daddies.

The first daddy, the one that everyone sees, is a nice daddy. He cares about people and is smiley and kind. I don't see him often, but he is busy looking after other people. People like that daddy, and I think I would too, if it wasn't for the other one...

It's quite confusing, really, because the other daddy looks the same and talks the same. He tells me that he loves me and that I'm his precious little girl. The trouble is, while he is saying those things, he is hurting me and making me feel dirty. I don't want love from this daddy. I don't like him or what he does to me.

Whenever he comes close to me, I always hope it's going to be the nice daddy, but then I often find out too late that it's the nasty daddy, who is too big and heavy for me to push away.

Because I can't trust the bad daddy, I can't trust the good one either. I can never tell them apart until it is too late

My good daddy is a minister, and he tells everyone about God.

Everyone tells me that God is a good father who we should love and trust. But I am just as confused about Him as I am about my real daddy. There's the God-daddy who everyone tells me loves me and wants me to be happy. They say I can trust Him, that He will always look after me. He is all-powerful. He sees everything that happens to me. All I have to do is pray and trust Him. If I am a good girl, then He will answer my prayers. But then, there's the other one. I cry out to Him, I pray to Him, and I try to be as good as I can so He will listen to my prayers. I know that if He wanted to, He could change things because He is all-powerful. But He doesn't. He has got the power, but He chooses not to help me. He must be up there laughing at me, enjoying watching me suffer, knowing He could change things but getting some kind of sick power kick from not doing so.

I am so very confused.

Everyone is telling me my real daddy could never have done those awful things to me. So why has the God-daddy let me have all those 'memories' if they aren't real? Is it the God-daddy that is really the bad one? Has He let me 'remember' all those things because He has enjoyed watching me suffer and go through hell, letting me be traumatised over and over again, only to turn around and say, "Just kidding – I let you give Me your 100% trust, so I thought I would abuse it just to make Me feel a bit more powerful!"

Everyone is so adamant my real daddy is the good daddy and not the bad daddy. The only way I can make sense of all this is to decide that my God-daddy, who I thought was the good daddy, is really the bad one.

I am so confused. How do I know which one is which?

I am hurting so badly. I feel completely broken. I just want to find someone I can trust.

I want someone to help me untangle this web of confusion.

I want someone to hold me together while I fall apart and feel all this pain.

But I can't find anyone who believes me when I talk about the bad daddy. They all believe in the good one. They also all believe in the good God-daddy. But I can't believe in both. Even when I convince myself that both daddies are the good daddy, as soon as I am in church and try to worship God, I get a tightness around my throat, memories of the bad daddy come flooding back, and I just get totally overwhelmed with emotion.

I am just going to have to walk away, stop going to church, stop believing there could be a good God-daddy who loves me because it's all just far too confusing and overwhelming. I can't make sense of any of it anymore ...

MJA, 1994

Chapter 5

The Girl On The Bookcase - Introducing The Six-Year-Old Me

I am in my bedroom. It's pitch-black dark.

I'm sitting on top of the bookcase, looking over to my bed. A big dark shadow is lying on top of my little body.

I have no idea what horror occurred on that night, but I know it was so awful that my spirit had to detach itself and leave my body so I could be an observer rather than a participant in whatever was being done to me.

I have never been able to visualise myself getting back into my body and allowing myself to experience whatever was happening.

Whenever I try to "connect" with my six-year-old self, she is still sitting on top of the bookcase.

She actually seems quite content to be there, detached and just watching on, like watching a horror movie with eyes glazed, not really taking in what she is watching because her brain just can't process what her eyes are seeing…

Chapter 6

The Girl In The Sumo Suit - Introducing The Eight-Year-Old Me

It took a very long time, probably two years of therapy sessions before I could even talk about my eight-year-old self.

Every time I thought about her, I felt sick. If I ever saw a photo of her, I was totally repulsed and disgusted with her. I hated her. I would scream at my counsellor that I wanted nothing to do with her, and if I was pressed as to why, I would end up with my head down the toilet, retching my guts up.

Whereas I wanted to be "reconnected" with some of the younger children, the thought of accepting her as "part of me" was utterly unthinkable, I often shouted with sheer venom that "I would rather die than have anything to do with her!"

She was having to deal with so much more than just the sexual abuse from her father. I am not going to share the additional ordeals she had to go through here because it is just too difficult.

I can, however, describe how she was feeling at that time.

She was beginning to realise that she was different from her friends.

She knew there was something fundamentally wrong with her; she wasn't feeling the way she was because of "the things being done to her"; rather, those things were happening to her because she was made wrong. She deserved all of those bad things. In the depths of her being, she believed that she was made of nothing but shit. She felt unlovable. Unacceptable. Unlikeable.

She was constantly being told by her mum that no one would love her until she got thin. She had already been on obsessive, highly restrictive, calorie-controlled diets for over two years. But she was also going on secret, uncontrollable binges. It was, therefore, her own fault she was so unlovable.

I now understand that she was actually surrounding herself with an emotional "sumo suit" of protection. The linings of the sumo suit held all the guilt, repulsion, disgust, filth, and layers and layers and layers of toxic shame that had been thrust upon her.

This is why whenever I saw a photo of her, thought about her, or tried to talk to my counsellor about her, all of those overpowering feelings of repulsion were triggered.

I thought she *was* those things. It took me a very long time to realise that this wasn't who she was – that underneath the sumo suit was a pure, innocent, beautiful, blameless, confused, frightened little girl worthy of love, affection and protection.

It took me even longer to realise that the sumo suit saved my life. If I had not projected all the anger, guilt, hatred, repulsion, disgust, filth and toxic shame onto myself and my body and instead tried to dump it where it really belonged, if I had fought it off and tried to push it back onto the people it belonged to rather than absorbing it all, I could have suffered far more than I actually did, and as a result, may well have died.

When I hear of teenagers now killing themselves because they had tried to tell people what was happening to them, but those around did not pick up the messages or did not believe them, it makes me extremely grateful for my sumo suit, grateful that my eight-year-old self had eating disorders, and later on, my teenage years developed even more dysfunctional behaviours such as self-harm. Those behaviours were part of an innate survival strategy. The pressure would have made me implode without them, and I would not have survived.

I remember the exact day and circumstances when my eight-year-old self realised that the "love" she received from both her parents was very different from the love her friends experienced. I had been unwell, and one of my friend's mums looked after me for the afternoon. As I lay on her sofa, I felt genuine care, compassion, and love for the first time ever, and I realised what I had been missing out on.

This created a "black hole" inside of me, a seemingly eternal vacuum of desolation and isolation. I was consumed with desperation to feel loved and accepted.

But the sumo suit I had constructed to protect me from the wrong kind of love had no filter. Even when I did come into contact with the right kind of love, it could not make its way through the thick, impenetrable layers of my self-protective suit of armour.

DADDY'S GIRL (age eight)

I want to be a "daddy's girl",
To feel the warmth of his love,
To see his eyes sparkle as he looks at me,
To feel safe as he gives me a hug.

I want to be my "daddy's girl",
To be his special child;
To know he's there to protect me.
And will never let go of my hand.

I would like to be a "daddy's girl",
To share lots of secrets and fun,
To know that whatever happens to me
I have a father to whom I can turn.

I want to be my "daddy's girl",
To look up to him with respect,
To know that no matter what I do
I'm a child he will never reject.

I want to be a "daddy's girl",
To have someone I can trust;
Someone to teach me how to get through,
And guide me when I am lost...

I suppose I am a "daddy's girl",
But in a vastly different way;
A way that fills me with despair,
And makes me want to die.

I hate being my "daddy's girl",
- the way it makes me feel inside;
All the secrets I have to keep,
The games and all the lies.

The only times I'm a "daddy's girl",
I am full of confusion and fear;
I end up feeling horrible,
Whenever he comes near.

The times I'm a "special daddy's girl",
I end up feeling hurt;
Whenever he tells me that I'm "daddy's girl".
My insides get torn apart.

When he says that I'm "daddy's girl".
And I see that look in his eyes,
I think I could vomit a hundred miles,
I just want to scream and cry.

They tell me that God wants me to be His "daddy's girl",
That He wants me to know His love;
He wants to show me how it should have been,
And teach me how to trust.

He wants me to know what it's like to jump,
And be caught in His strong, safe arms;
He wants to show me a love that won't hurt,
To feel special without being harmed.

I desperately want to be God's "daddy's girl",
To be His precious one;
To know it's OK to have some love
Without it feeling wrong.

I long to be God's "daddy's girl",
To find out what it's like
To be loved and made to feel special,
Without a massive fight.

To feel that there is somewhere I belong,
And someone I can trust;
To know there is someone to whom I can turn
Without being subjected to their lust.

I really want to be God's "daddy's girl",
But I don't know if it's worth the risk,
Of reliving the pain and confusion
And the betrayal that comes with a kiss.

I'd like to be God's "daddy's girl",
But I don't know if I can;
I don't know if I can take the chance,
Because He reminds me so much of a man.

I want to feel His gentle touch,
To experience love without fear;
But instead, I'm filled with guilt, disgust and shame,
Whenever I let Him near.

I want to be God's "daddy's girl".
And to know His Father's heart,
To feel pure love and acceptance,
The way it should have felt from the start.

I wish I could be God's "daddy's girl";
It is really my greatest desire,
To dare to believe He won't do me more harm -
But it's too much like playing with fire.

So, I don't think I can be God's "daddy's girl,"
At least, not for today,
However, as much as I want to be safe in His arms,
It feels far safer to run away

MJA, 1993

Chapter 7

The Thunderstorm – Introducing The Ten-Year-Old Me

I have always had an irrational fear of thunderstorms. I am gripped by sheer terror at the sound of thunder.

When my grandad came to stay for the summer holidays, I slept in the spare room at the back of the house. I read one of Enid Blyton's "Famous Five" books. All the children were fast asleep during a raging storm. They were oblivious to the impending danger about to befall them. Lightning hit a tree, and as the tree started falling towards the house where the children were sleeping, Timmy the dog started barking and ran into the room to wake them up. Hearing the sound of the falling tree, the children all ran out of the room just as it came crashing through the house. If it wasn't for Timmy, the dog, they would have been crushed to death!!!

I spent hours looking out of the window of the spare bedroom and calculated that the tree between our back garden and the neighbours could definitely kill me in the same way in a thunderstorm!

Into my adulthood, I continued to tell myself this was the reason for my irrational fear of storms. I was in my mid-forties, during a particularly terrifying storm, that I allowed myself to see there was more to my story.

Around the time I was eight, my mum passed her driving test and got a job as a district nurse. No more night duty. Because of this, I'd had a reprieve. I don't think I have any memories (good or bad) between the ages of nine and ten, apart from one…

It is the summer of 1976, the "year of the drought" in the UK, with lots of very hot, humid nights. I'm sleeping in the spare room when I'm woken up by a loud clap of thunder. I immediately run to my mum and dad's bedroom, without remembering that my mum is away (I have no idea why she wasn't there). Fortunately, both of my brothers had beaten me to it and were already in the room with my father. While the storm raged, we chatted and counted the seconds between the thunderclap and the lightning to work out how far away the storm was. I don't know how long we were there, but I was too busy counting on my brothers to be frightened.

Until the storm passed.

My father sent my brothers back to their room. I was about to follow, but he insisted I stay.

I don't have any clear memories of what happened next. But every time I remember that night and my brothers leaving the room, my abdomen gets such intense knots of anxiety searing through it; I end up wanting to throw up, and my whole body starts to shake.

The same thing still happens now whenever there is a thunderstorm.

Behind Closed Doors

How many children behind those closed doors
Enduring things that will never be seen?
How many screams hiding behind those smiles?
How many uncried tears?

How much fear disguised by those sparkling eyes?
How much pain do they hide?
What trauma is disguised by singing those happy songs?
Stories that can never be told?

How long, oh God, until something is done?
How long until justice prevails?
How long until children can sit safely on a knee?
How long, oh God, how long?

How long, oh God, until love can flow
To each little one living in fear?
How long until all the dark secrets are exposed?
How long, oh God, how long?

Only you see what goes on behind those closed doors;
The violation and the pain,
Small eyes watching things that should go unseen,
Innocence lost and never regained.

Young shoots trampled before they begin to bud,
Hearts broken as trust is betrayed,
Young lives lost before they have time to grow;
Their beauty submerged by their pain

How long, oh God, until something is done?
How long until justice prevails?
How long until children can sit safely on a knee?
How long, Oh God, how long?

How long, oh God, until love can flow
To each little one living in fear?
How long until all the dark secrets are exposed?
How long, Oh God, how long?

When, Oh God, will you break down those closed doors
And let your children go free?
When will the chains of wickedness be loosed?
So, they can be who you created them to be?

How long until light shines into all those dark rooms
And love reaches in to save?
When, oh when, will anyone care enough
To rescue those innocent slaves?

How long, oh God, until something is done?
How long until justice prevails?
How long until children can sit safely on a knee?
How long, oh God, how long?

How long, oh God, until love can flow
To each little one living in fear?
How long until all the dark secrets are exposed?
How long, Oh God, how long?

MJA 16.2.98

Chapter 8

Living Inside The Pig's Carcass; Introducing My Teenage Years

I don't really have any significant traumatic memories between the ages of ten and thirteen. I was bumbling around in my sumo suit, still feeling fat and frustrated with myself; my mum was still putting me on a new diet every few weeks but they all failed miserably because of my uncontrollable binging, which had become bulimic (making myself sick at the end of every binge).

I started secondary school just after my thirteenth birthday. I hated it. I desperately tried to make friends, but they were all growing into young women, getting more attractive, talking about hair, makeup, and boyfriends. I just didn't fit in. I hated myself. I hated my body. I hated being at school, but I also hated being at home. I tried to get thin, making sure I never ate more than 300 – 400 calories every day, but then, at least once a week, I was going on massive, secret binges, sabotaging my own efforts and getting more and more angry with myself on every occasion.

I hated being around my family, so I spent more and more time in my room. I spent two hours a day playing my flute and the rest of the time doing schoolwork.

But something far, far more significant also happened at that time.

My mum became pregnant, and my baby brother was born just before my thirteenth birthday. Before this, my mum was still working dayshifts as a nurse. But in September, I started secondary school, and she went back to working nights. She worked every Saturday night and often did a second night during the week.

My friends started to go out on Saturday nights and, on several occasions, invited me to parties. My mum wouldn't let me go. Instead, she made me stay in and do house chores. Every Saturday night, while my father worked on his sermons or watched TV and my brothers did their own thing, I was on my hands and knees washing the kitchen floor, cleaning the oven or looking after the baby. The traditional gender roles were firmly entrenched - the females in the family ran around cleaning up all the men's shit while they did whatever the fuck they liked.

Once again, my father had "free access" to me. My reprieve was over.

I have no words to fully describe the internal world of my teenagers. Even now, almost three years into the counselling process, when I go into sessions intending to talk about some of my experiences during those years, I sit in silence, or I go into a 'deep freeze" state where I feel I have gone under general anaesthetic and all I can do is curl up in the tightest ball I can, in the corner of the room furthest away from my counsellor and as close to the door as possible.

During my first year of secondary school, I rebelled. I had already developed an image of God as someone who was all-powerful, who could see what was going on in my life, could see how unhappy I was, who could hear me crying out every time my mum and dad went out in the car, praying with all my might that they would be killed in a car crash so I could live in a different family. But God did not answer my prayers. He must have been getting some kind of power kick out of watching me suffer.

My mum was still telling me the cause of all my problems was because I was fat, and all I had to do for my friends to like me and for others to love me was to get thin. Yet, at the same time, people would tell me that diets wouldn't make any difference; if I was fat, it was because "God made me that way". In other words, God made me unlovable!

I did everything I could to rebel. I tried to be angry. I swore. I started smoking. Although I wasn't allowed to stop attending church, I stopped going to Guides and the Sunday night youth fellowship after church. But the more I tried to rebel, the more my parents piled on the guilt. Despite all of my rebellion, I still didn't fit in anywhere. I felt isolated, lonely, and misunderstood.

When I was thirteen and a half, I had serious thoughts of suicide. I told a friend at church one Sunday evening. She told her mum, who said she would ring and talk to my mum. I clearly remember the following day. I couldn’t concentrate at school. I remember cycling home feeling a glimpse of hope – at last, my mum was going to see how unhappy I was; she would talk to me and listen to how much I hated myself. She would understand just how depressed I was, and she would find some way of helping me.

But instead, as soon as I came in the door, she sat me down at the kitchen table, became very cross, and told me off. She said there was nothing wrong with me and that I was just attention-seeking. She then made me pray with her to ask God for forgiveness for being so bad.

Not only did I feel even more despair, but I was also devoid of all hope, knowing I couldn't talk to my friends or youth leaders anymore because my mum had told them all to ignore me because I was just attention-seeking.

In July of that year, there was a "Don Summers Crusade" in a big-top tent for a week. He was an American evangelist (a small-scale Billy Graham), and all the churches in town had been planning this for months. I wasn't interested, but after getting away with not going for most of the week, I was forced to go on the last night.

Towards the end of the evening, when they started playing all this emotional music and gave a big appeal for people to turn back to God, the anger and rebellion I had been feeling for most of that year dissolved, and I was once again consumed with feeling dark, dirty, filthy, unlovable and enveloped in layers and layers of deep shame.

I went forward to pray with someone, ask for forgiveness, and end my rebellion. I wanted to feel clean, forgiven, acceptable, and loveable.

I "prayed the prayer".

But it changed nothing. No amount of praying changed what was happening to me or how it made me feel.

Walking Down the Street

Walking down the street, I hear the church bells ringing,
Sounding out the tune of a well-known hymn;
Smartly dressed people walking to church,
Going to praise a God they think is real.

Who is this God? I'm so confused.
Has He anything to offer to me?
Don't understand. Can't make it out.
Can someone please tell me –
What is it all about?

I switch on the TV; the news is all bad.
Another bomb in Ireland and another soldier was killed.
All the war and hatred that's in the world today
Yet people say it's all part of "God's perfect plan."

Who is this God? I'm so confused.
Has He anything to offer to me?
Don't understand. Can't make it out.
Can someone please tell me –
What is it all about?

Some say God is real, but is it all imagination?
Is He just an old man in the sky?
Was Jesus just a good man, or was He the Son of God?
Is He dead, or is He really "reigning on high?"

Who is this God? I'm so confused.
Has He anything to offer to me?
Don't understand. Can't make it out.
Can someone please tell me –
What is it all about?

They say God made the earth and all of creation
But I don't know why He made me.
Life seems so pointless, such a waste of time.
I'm drowning in such darkness I can't see.

Who is this God? I'm so confused.
Has He anything to offer to me?
Don't understand. Can't make it out.
Can someone please tell me –
What is it all about?

MJH 11.9.81 (age 15)
AIMtogetbetter2024

Like a Lost Child

Like a lost child in the middle of a busy street,
I don't know where to go, which way to turn,
I don't know what I'm doing here.
I'm sure I don't fit in
I'm trapped in a prison;
It's called the prison of life.

They say that God made me, that this is part of His plan,
But He's locked me in a dungeon and thrown away the key.
He's supposed to be all-powerful,
But He's playing a sick game.
He's trapped me in a prison;
It's called the prison of life.

I'm lost in a maze, but there's no way of getting out,
There's nowhere to go and nowhere to turn.
I know I shouldn't be here,
It's all one big mistake
But I'm trapped in the prison;
It's called the prison of life.

MJH 20.9.81 (aged 15)

Fed Up and Hungry (Age 15)

I'm stuck in a world that no one understands,
Misunderstood and alone.
I'm not the same as any of my friends;
My heart is made of stone.

No matter what I do on the outside
To be normal and OK
On the inside, I stay abnormal,
Disgusting and afraid.

Afraid that no one can love me,
That no one can really care
Afraid to let anyone near me
In case they see what's really there.

Although on the outside, I try to be "me"
A "me" I think people will like
On the inside, it's different; it's disgusting, it smells,
Completely obnoxious, like something from hell.

No matter how much I try to pretend and ignore it,
I know on the inside, there's nothing but shit.
I know my Mum loves me, that she knows something is wrong,
But she ignores the real reason and can't admit what's going on.

She knows that I'm abnormal and can see I don't fit in
But instead of facing the real problem, she blames me for not being thin.

After years of loads of diets, the problem is getting worse
The shit inside is spreading, so much of it I'm going to burst.
Why won't she look deeper? Why can't I make her see
That the things that are really happening are on the inside of me?

I need her to see what's going on,
The poison that's spreading inside
That's infecting every part of me,
If she doesn't, I'm going to die.

She's convinced herself that the only thing wrong
Is that I'm unhappy because I'm not thin!
So, I'll get anorexic, I'll start hating food
I'll make sure I don't eat another thing.

When she sees I'm still sad even after I'm thin
Then maybe she will see;
Maybe then she'll take a deeper look
And see what's happening to me.

But when I stop eating, she makes my life hell
The problem now is that I'm making myself ill;
The solution is to have something nice to eat
I'll soon feel better if she buys me a treat!!

How can I get through to her
That the issues are more than skin deep?
How can I ever make her see
That the problem is not what I eat?

If she thinks that I'm unhappy
Because I don't eat a single thing
Then I'll go the other way completely
I'll do nothing but binge and binge.

I'll have all the things that she says are nice,
I'll do nothing but stuff and stuff;
Then, when I'm still miserable
She'll realise that nice food isn't enough.

But now I have to be careful
To make sure I don't get fat
Because as soon as I do, she'll notice,
And then start blaming that.

So, whatever I eat
I must purge myself clean
Whatever I put in,
I must get straight out again.
It doesn't matter how I do it,
Or what it does to my health;
I won't notice how much I vomit
Or how much I hurt myself.

I've just got to show her,
I'm desperate for her to see,
That the issue isn't my body,
That the real problem is me.

Why can't she see I'm fed up,
Not with food, but with my inner dirt?
Why does she insist on staying so blind
To how much my insides hurt?

I'm getting frustrated, I start to despair.
Will I ever find a way to show her what's really in here?
I start to get angry and do what I can to rebel
I shout, and I swear, and I make her life hell.

But now, the only problem she sees
Is that because I'm so bad, God has stopped loving me!
I'll soon be happy if I repent and apologise,
When, tell me when, will she open her eyes?

Now I've taken too much, I want to run and hide
I decide the only solution left is committing suicide.
My last hope is to tell her I want to die.
But she just tells me off for telling such lies.

She says I'm attention-seeking,
Just playing silly games.
I now have no one to turn to,
Misunderstood, rejected again.

So, I'll give up,
Stop wanting anyone to care
I'll push away anyone
Who tries to come near.

I'll non-exist, make the real me hide,
I'll never feel anything on the inside.
I'll forget what's in there or where it came from.
On the outside, I'll pretend, but on the inside, I'll die.

MJA March 1994

The Dress and the Dog Collar (Age Fifteen and A Half)

It's Sunday night. I still have my Sunday best dress on. I remember it vividly – I had recently lost quite a lot of weight and, for the first time I can remember, felt really good and "grown up" in this dress. I can remember the colour and the patterns on it…

…I'm in Mum and Dad's bedroom, lying on the bed. My father is on top of me. He is still wearing his dog collar.

I have no idea why he is wearing his dog collar. In the last few years, he has mostly only worn a suit and tie on Sundays—the dog collar only came out at funerals and a few very special occasions.

I also have no idea why my mum wasn't there as she tended to work Saturdays, not Sundays.

This is one of the memories which I remember vividly, with every one of my senses. I can smell the smell of his dog collar and his sweat, I can hear the words he is saying to me, I can feel the weight of him on top of me, and then, after I try to fight and push him off, the tightness around my throat as he leans his arm across my neck and uses his body weight to press down until I stop resisting because I can't breathe.

The memory is so visceral; every time I get the flashback, the smell of his dog collar is so vivid it causes a strong acidic stench in the back of my throat, and I automatically throw up violently.

There is something about this memory that I find impossible to put into words.

The fact that he is wearing his dog collar somehow has the same significance as the first seaside memory.

I have a profound sense of the perverseness of both situations… I had to live my whole life with the reality of this man's dual personality, wondering why he could represent such godliness, light, hope, grace, and freedom to everyone who knew him, yet he represented the complete opposite to me.

These two memories mess with my head more than any of the others.

They cause questions in the depth of my soul that I can't articulate and to which I know there will never be an answer.

The Power of My Father's Love

You come to me offering a rare chance of feeling wanted by you.
You come offering time and affection.
Offering me a chance to feel loved and cared for—an emotion I rarely get a chance to feel.
You know I want to feel love and acceptance and that I need to be affirmed by you.
I need you to give me a sense of being and acknowledge who I am.
I need to feel protected by you.
I need to feel that you are there to interpret meaning and show me where I fit into
this big, frightening, outside world that I don't understand.
So, I open myself up to you when you come to me.
I make myself vulnerable so that you can meet these needs of mine.
None of the frightening things around me that my mind is trying to make sense of can harm me when you are there.
I give you my trust.
I give you my vulnerability.
I show you my weaknesses and my need for protection.
When you come to me, I am open, exposed, and accepting of all you have to offer.

It is then that you strike.
When I have no protection, you pierce your 'sword' through me.
You show no mercy.
You cut ruthlessly through my body, my mind, my sense of being.
You rip open every part so there is no boundary between my sense of self and you; there is no border between my spirit and yours; my body is no longer mine as you penetrate it and make it merge with yours.
I am totally under your control.
You make the rules.
You have the power.

My sense of self is filled with you—I don't know what is me and what is you. I don't know what is love and what is pain. I don't know the difference between experiencing care and affection and being taken over and dominated.
I have no control.
You play the shots.
You decide when I am allowed to feel love and when, instead, I feel pain.
I never know when I open myself up to you and become vulnerable to you, whether you are going to fill me up with your love or your poison, whether you are going to affirm me or break me.
You decide.
You have the power.
You make the rules.
You take all the control.
Like your body thrusting in and out of mine, you give and take, offer love then pain, acceptance then desolation.

Not only do you make the rules, but you also change them to suit you.
But you don't tell me— I have to find out at my own expense.
I have no say in the rules you make.
I just have to play by them without even knowing what they are.

So now, my only way of taking any control back is to close myself up and cut myself off.
I will no longer make myself vulnerable to you.
I won't feel the pain if I don't open up to the love.
By taking away my openness, I take away your ability to hurt me.
I have no power over the rules you make, so instead, I will shut you out.
I will reject you.
I will take away your power to dominate me or affect me in any way.
I may not be able to stop you entering my body, but I will stop you from penetrating my soul.

Now, I cannot be hurt by you.
Now, you cannot dominate me.
Now, you cannot control me or the way I feel.
You cannot influence my inner being if I have not got one.
You cannot make me feel rejected if I no longer want your love.
You cannot cause me pain if I do not let you near me.
You cannot take advantage if I am no longer making myself vulnerable to you.

But I can only do this with you if I do it with everyone.
I will shut everyone out.
I will reject everyone who comes near.
I will not let anyone penetrate my soul.
I can't be hurt by anyone.
No one can dominate me or, control me or, cause me pain or come near.
No one will break my spirit if it is already dead.
Now, I am in control.
Now, I make the rules.
Now I have the power....
Now, I can survive.

MJA, 1993

Each memory I have from my teenage years has a far, far deeper impact on me than my childhood ones.

Maybe because I was more aware of what was going on?

Maybe because I felt I should have done something to stop it? Maybe I should have fought harder or screamed rather than freezing and zoning out?

But there is also another explanation.

Throughout my teenage years, from the very first time my mum spoke to me about love, relationships and sex, she was obsessive about one aspect – that it was imperative I never had sex with anyone until I married. I had to remain a virgin until my wedding day, and once married, I could only ever have sex with my husband. Intercourse and any other kind of sexual activity were strictly forbidden outside of marriage, and if any man who wanted to marry me found out that I wasn't a virgin, he would not want to marry me because I would be physically and spiritually tarnished.

But that wasn't all.

She also repeatedly told me that the responsibility to ensure that no sexual activity took place before marriage belonged solely to the woman. If a couple did enter into any kind of sexual activity outside of marriage, it was always the woman who was to blame because men "just can't help themselves". No man was able to have any control over their sexual desires when they were alone with a woman, so it was always up to the woman to make sure nothing sinful happened.

She didn't just tell me this once or twice – she went on and on about it. Why did she keep banging on about it over and over again?

When I spoke about this for the first time to my counsellor, the reality dawned on me that maybe she subconsciously knew what was going on, and she was pinning the blame on me.

The impact of these teenage experiences is that the sumo suit had been replaced with a huge, fat, disgusting pig carcass, which I carried with me all of the time, wherever I went. I was consumed with the stench of its rotting entrails and thought others could smell the noxious smell whenever I came near them. As my bulimia became extreme, there were times when I had my head down the toilet, and I was violently forcing my hands down my throat, that I actually saw my hands turning into pig trotters, and the sound of me catching my breath in between my retching was the sound of a ravenous hog snorting. I felt I deserved nothing better than to be sent to the abattoir to be slowly and painfully slaughtered.

Until very recently, if I was ever reminded of my teenagers or saw photos of them, I had the same visceral reaction that I had with the eight-year-old, but the self-abhorrence, self-disgust, repulsion, guilt, and toxic shame were even more forceful.

Trying to find healing for these teenagers is a very slow process.

Chapter 9

The Game - Introducing My Sixteen-Year-Old Self

Two months after my sixteenth birthday, I was admitted to an acute psychiatric ward, having made several serious attempts on my life.

I had been in a very, very dark place for many months.

My first overdose was serious enough for me to be admitted to the hospital. I have no idea how long I was there, but the first thing I remember when I woke up, still attached to a drip, was my mum and dad sitting next to me. My mum appeared genuinely upset. My father just told me that no one must ever know what I had done and that if anyone found out I had done this, it would go against me for the rest of my life because there was such a stigma associated with being mentally ill.

The evening I returned home from the hospital, our GP visited me. He was a friend of my parents and an elder in the Plymouth Brethren Church (all I know about that church is that, at that time, they were even more conservative in their beliefs than the Baptists). My parents left me alone with him. I thought he was going to talk to me, listen and understand. Instead, he got his Bible out and read Psalm 139 to me, and then spent what seemed like an eternity preaching at me about what a terrible, terrible sin it was to try and take your own life, and the chances were that anyone who committed suicide would go to hell. I'm not sure what he or my parents were trying to achieve through this, but whatever it was, it didn't work. I did not suddenly stop wanting to die. It just made me more determined than ever that, when I did kill myself, I needed to make damn sure that I went to hell; I was far, far more frightened of the remote possibility that I may still get into heaven!

The Game

I'm playing a game. It's quite simple: hide-and-seek.
But there's something different about the way I'm playing compared to the way it's usually played because I'm playing it with God, and the prize at stake is my life.
I've been playing the game for some years now. Most of the time, I'm looking for God, trying to find Him, trying to reach Him. But He's much better at the game than I am, and He's very good at hiding, so good that I haven't found Him yet.
I often get near to where He is - I've been so near that I could feel His presence, I could know that my searching was nearly over, that all I had to do was reach out my hand and....
... and suddenly, He's gone! No longer there. He's run away again so that I can't find Him.
Then, the game starts all over again. I start searching, shouting, and crying, experiencing the same feelings of anger, frustration, and loneliness that I've felt so many times before.
The worst thing about it is that wherever I go, I feel that it isn't me seeking God, but Him following me, watching every movement, hearing me when I call, aware of what I'm feeling and what I'm going through, enjoying my frustration, teasing me by letting me get close then running away, laughing at me going round and round in circles.

In the end, I get too tired to play, too frustrated, and too disillusioned—why bother playing when I can never win?
At this point, I decide to hide—to run away as far as I can, shouting, "OK, God, it's your turn to find me!" I make it as hard as I can for Him; I hide in dark places. I put on elaborate disguises and bury myself in places I think He won't think of looking. I try to forget about Him, thinking that if I forget about Him, He will forget about me and stop looking for me.
But He doesn't play the game according to the rules. When I hide, He doesn't bother coming to find me. He just watches. And laughs.

He doesn't have to come and find me because He always knows where I am. He spoils the game.
I often think I've got away from Him, but He comes along again as soon as I do. He never comes and finds me or pulls me out of my hiding place. He comes just close enough for me to know He's there; never close enough for me to touch Him or feel His love, just close enough to torture me, make me realise that He is powerful enough to make up the rules as He goes along. He is playing with me the way a cat plays with a mouse because He enjoys watching me suffer. This makes me angry, frustrated, confused. He gets much closer to other people than He does me; they often say how wonderful, loved, and accepted it makes them feel, but I never feel any of that.
I often shout out, "OK, God, it's your turn. Come and find me!" But He never does.
Maybe the reality is that I don't want to be found? Maybe I'm too scared? Too scared, in case he does come close enough for me to feel His love. In case, one day, He gets close enough to see what I'm really like and, rejects me and walks away for good. Or, even worse, He sees what I'm really like and continues to love me anyway. I couldn't cope with that. I'm too frightened to let anyone close enough. I have to keep hiding, because whenever I feel love I also feel extreme fear and pain. I just can't take the risk.
So, I'm going to stop playing. For good. I know it is breaking the rules, but I'm going to have to cheat.
But I'm frightened. Not about killing myself, that bit seems easy. But what if I kill myself and don't go to hell? What if I end up in heaven, facing Him and His love, but with nowhere to hide or run away? I'd spend eternity wanting to get away, run, and be back on earth so I can hide away again – anything, anything so I don't have to feel His love.

I can't risk it. I can't risk ending up in heaven. I'm going to have to keep playing the game until I can find a way to guarantee I will go to hell or find a way to run far enough away to be safe from His love. Only then can I stop playing the game for good.

MJA Oct '82.

In the days following that first overdose, I felt trapped. I was completely broken. I knew I couldn't go on. The only thing I wanted to do was die. I could think about nothing else, day or night. I hated my parents. I hated myself. I hated my body. I hated my life. But most of all, I hated God.

I'm not too sure what happened over the next few days, but I was visited at home by a psychiatrist who insisted I be admitted to the psychiatric hospital. This was long before there were any specialist services for children and young people, so I was admitted to a ward full of women of all ages.

I remember that first evening clearly. As I sat in a corner of the day room, I observed Margaret, probably in her mid-fifties, walking around backwards with her handbag on her head. There was an older woman called Dorothy sitting in the corner with her coat on, a scarf on her head and fag hanging out of her mouth, saying over and over again, "They're all fuckin mad; all of them are completely fuckin mad!" Later on, a lady called Janice, who was in her mid-thirties, came in. She was ever so excitable and chatty, then laughed as she told me she had just met up with an 18-year-old patient from the men's ward next door and had sex with him in the bushes outside! I didn't understand why such a cheerful, happy person was locked up in the hospital (I now realise she had bipolar disorder).

As a frightened sixteen-year-old, I wondered why I had been locked up in here with all these mad people. Maybe I was mad, too?

I spent weeks on 1:1 nursing as I was so suicidal. Despite having a nurse to myself, I spent all my time curled up in a corner of the room, not eating, not sleeping, not talking. All I wanted to do was die and go to hell. If the nurses tried to encourage me to "talk about my problems" my only response was, "I'm the problem. There's something wrong with me. The only way to solve my problems is let me kill myself and get rid of me."

I remember thinking there was one advantage to being in the hospital: now everyone in the church would know I was here. Maybe it would make them realise we weren't the perfect minister's family, and maybe they would start to ask why and see through the façade. Maybe someone would come to visit and genuinely want to find out what had made me so sad.

Instead, the first time my father came to visit, he had made a list of about four people (his friends, not mine) who could come and visit me and gave the nurses very strict instructions that under no circumstances was anyone else allowed to visit. He told me that this was for my protection, to stop nosey people visiting and gossiping about it later.

What I didn't realise at the time was that he was telling people in the church that I was extremely mentally ill and needed to be left alone while I had the necessary treatment.

As the weeks went on, my psychiatrist and the nursing staff kept telling me that I wasn't ill, that it wasn't normal for a sixteen-year-old girl to be in such a state of despair and self-hatred, so there must have been something going on inside the family for me to be the way I was. At the same time, when my parents visited, they continued to tell me that I was seriously mentally ill and just needed to let the doctors make me better.

Who was I meant to believe?

My psychiatrist insisted on setting up a family therapy session just for me, my mum, and my father. I was adamant it wouldn't work, but he insisted. When it came to the day, my father turned up on his own. Apparently, my baby brother had chicken pox (which miraculously only lasted one day). I don’t know if my mum just couldn't face it or whether my father engineered this so that, if I had disclosed any of his abuse, my mum wouldn’t be there to hear it.

The doctor suggested I start by talking about some things that upset me at home. I went for relatively neutral topics. Whatever I brought up, my father put on his most pious, patronising Baptist minister’s voice and denied everything, blatantly lying and telling me that I was the one making everything up and imagining things. Something inside me snapped. It was obvious he would rather me rot inside an asylum than ever, ever admit that he could have done something wrong. I walked out of the room, more determined than ever that I just needed to die.

That evening, I made yet another attempt to kill myself, which led to me getting restrained by four members of staff and being taken to the “padded room” where I had an injection in my bum.

But rather than that experience causing me even more trauma, while I was being held down, I felt something I had never felt before; I felt safe. For the first time ever, someone cared enough to intervene to prevent me from coming to harm. I was being held and "contained" as I screamed and raged and got relief from emotions that had been pent up inside me for years. Whatever it was that I felt in that moment, it set into motion a pattern of "emotionally addictive" behaviour that would dominate my life for the next twenty-five years.

Over the next few months, I had several failed discharges – mainly due to the fact that, although the doctors and nurses responsible for my treatment knew that something was going on at home, I was discharged back into the care of my parents. Towards the end of my third admission, I knew that I would rather die than go back home. So, I got a full-time job, and the social workers started looking for a place to live.

The night I went to tell my parents I was not coming back home to live, all hell let loose. My mum cried, and my father shouted with a rage I had never seen from him before or since. During this heated exchange, he said something that confirmed my suspicions; he would rather I was locked up in the hospital forever and let everyone think I was mad, or better still, kill myself than ever admit to himself or anyone else that any of my issues were down to him. As he said it, I felt something inside me snap, as if my spirit was completely torn. I fell silent, turned around, and walked out of the house without saying a word or feeling anything.

Behind Your Mask

All I can see is your minister's face,
Your caring Christian smile,
You've gained so much love and respect from your flock,
You have really done it so well.

But are you happy behind that façade?
What do you feel behind that brick wall?
Are you convincing yourself, as well as the rest?
Do you enjoy trying to deceive them all?

How would you cope if you revealed to the world
The man behind the gown and the collar?
If you took off your disguise and your impenetrable mask,
Could you bear to lose your respectable image?

Why don't you show who's really in there
- the reality behind the cloth?
Why can't you admit it's all a big con;
An effort to give you self-worth

Go on, show them who you really are;
They wouldn't believe their eyes!
Show them the man who screws his four-year-old child,
Then makes her keep it secret with emotional bribes.

If only you could hear the silent screams
Resounding from the depths of my being,
If only you'd allow yourself to feel
Just a fraction of the pain I'm feeling.

Do you know what it's like to be so misunderstood,
For no one to see your pain?
Do you know what it's like to have your insides torn apart
While someone gently whispers your name?

If only you would allow yourself to face
The truth and reality;
If only you would reach out and take my hand
As I attempt to face the past honestly.

But I know you won't do it - you won't take off your mask
It's too hard for you to do
So, I'll sit back and laugh as you play all your games
Because I know the real you.

MJH Nov '82

During my third admission, I started receiving letters from a family friend whom I had known all my life. He was five or six years older than me. His letters made me smile and gave me a glimmer of hope. We became close, and the lifeline he offered me was enough for me to make plans to move closer to him and start a college course.

So, You're Feeling Bad

So, you're feeling bad; all you want to do is die.
You can't cope with life; all that you can do is cry.
No one understands you, no one even seems to try,
They all think you want attention,
When all you want to do is die......

So, you hate yourself, there's nothing in you that's good,
You're one big failure; you'd change in any way you could.
You don't believe anyone loves you, you don't know why anyone cares,
You want them all to hate you,
You turn your back on everyone that's there.........

"Pull yourself together, girl." You couldn't do it if you tried.
You're too afraid to fight; your only hope is suicide
You think they can all just forget you, forget you were ever there,
You don't think anyone would notice
If you curled up and simply disappeared ....

I am here for you, standing by your side
It might be hard for you, but you can do it if you try
Just accept the help I offer, reach out and take my hand
You can learn to live again, learn again to stand

Yes, you can learn to live again, make your life worthwhile
You can learn to love again, learn again to smile.
Yes, you can learn to laugh again, as you learn that life is worthwhile,
You can learn to hope again, learn again to smile.

MJH 19th Dec 1982

Dedicated to Phil, who gave me hope (and Smarties) at a time when I needed it the most.

Chapter 10

Stuck In Emotional Addiction - My Adult Years

After spending most of my "gap year" in the hospital, I spent the next twenty years going around in endless, frustrating circles, gaining qualifications, becoming a very confident and competent nurse, a qualified clinical trainer, and a public health specialist sometimes contributing to department of health strategies; but just as I felt I had built my life back up, something inside me would "click" and I would resort back to my self-destructive behaviours, often leading to more admissions to hospital, sometimes losing jobs and relationships along the way.

I could not control the behaviours once I had clicked back into them. For years, the anger, frustration, guilt and shame I piled on myself because of my own behaviours paralleled the feelings piled on me by others during my childhood.

Over time, I was able to identify patterns, but I still felt powerless to stop it from happening again and again.

I would meet a nice, kind, caring woman (the opposite of my mum), either at church or through work. I would develop a friendship. I would tell them about my depression, eating disorders and self-harm and would feel love and compassion in response. This would rip open the chasm in my heart and once again expose the seemingly insatiable need for feminine love and affection.

For years, I wondered if I was gay, but no, I just needed a mum. But no sooner did I feel that maybe this person could fill the gaps inside my broken heart, chaos was let loose inside me as all of the children inside tried to burst out of me at once, all desperate to be noticed and tell their stories. I immediately felt out of control, and my behaviours would take over – the eating disorders, the self-harm, behaviours that many would call "attention seeking" (but I chose to call "emotional addiction"). As with any other addiction, rather than meeting the need by trying to satiate it, it just became greater; the behaviours always escalated until I ended up back in the hospital.

The relationship often came to an end, sometimes because I sucked out every ounce of emotional energy they had or was too demanding of their time when they often had young families of their own to look after, or because they just couldn't understand, or cope with, my distressing behaviours. Having found the hope of receiving the "mothering" I desperately longed for, it always ended with disappointment, isolation and rejection. As a result, I was living with chronic depression.

The Island

There's an island in the middle of the sea, in the middle of nowhere. Miles from anyone, miles from anything. Just one small, desolate, solitary island.

Not many people know that the island is there. To those who know of its meaningless existence, it is too far away, too unreachable.

It is possible that there may be a way to get to the island, but to most people, it can't be worth the effort. There is something about the island that no one understands: it is totally barren. Nothing grows there.

There used to be a few little shoots slowly growing, but some time ago, a storm washed them away. Now, there is nothing.

Occasionally, a small weed or shrub starts to grow again, but as soon as it does, another storm comes along and drowns it.

Sometimes, a storm isn't needed; a drop of rain is enough. Sometimes, it doesn't even need that; the weed just shrivels up of its own accord.

For some time now, the island has tried to produce artificial plants to cover up the barrenness, but even those get broken or washed away, revealing once more the nothingness that is really there.

No one understands the island. For some time, people have tried to work it out. They have put a lot of effort into trying to reach it. When they get there, they find nothing. Even experts have tried digging up the soil, testing it, and trying to find what it is made of to see if that gives any answer. But no one has found anything. Maybe they haven't dug deep enough. Maybe they can't dig anymore. Maybe they don't know what to do, so have they given up?

This dismal, insignificant island is a lost cause, not worth the time or effort to dig deep and find its hidden treasure.

Some may blame the island itself, saying it doesn't want to be reached or helped. If only they knew. If only they could see the danger, see the raging storm.

Now, not only have all the plants gone, but the island itself is disappearing, gradually sinking lower and lower, slowly breaking up under the waves.
Soon, the island will have gone. There will be no trace of it, no sign of its existence.
People may wonder about its disappearance, why it was ever here anyway, and what its purpose was.
Some will blame the island for not trying hard enough, not trying to fight; how selfish of it to give up and be broken into pieces so easily; it obviously didn't try.
Other people won't care. Most won't even know.
But one thing is for certain.
No one will ever know the pain, the heartache, the loneliness , or the battles that the island went through in its struggle to survive, its fight to exist and grow.........
ALL IN VAIN.

MJA 1985

At the age of 24, I engaged in regular sessions with a psychiatrist. She was one of the few people who continued to believe everything I told her at the time that my brother was convincing everyone else that I was making it all up. But after about a year, she went on maternity leave and never returned. The month she went on maternity leave, I married a man who believed he could "fix me". Unfortunately, he turned out to be an emotionally abusive "gas- lighter" and the marriage lasted just over two years.

The Island's Reprieve

It's a few years on, and against all the odds, the island is still there. It had continued to ebb away and had lost all traces of life. Every storm ripped more of it apart until it finally went completely under, totally submerged.

But then something strange happene Just as it seemed that it was destroyed completely, a specialist came along and started to rescue it. For some reason, they took an interest in the island. They dug deep until they found the reason for its barrenness. They discovered that years ago, when the island was beginning to form, the person in charge of looking after it and nurturing it injected it with poison. Not a poison that causes instant death, but one that slowly spreads, infecting every part at every level, so nothing could grow or flourish. No amount of sun, fertiliser, or planting seeds could make anything grow because this poison killed everything.

When the specialist discovered the poison, many of the people who had been trying to reach the island went away. Some turned away because they didn't want to get infected themselves, and some because they could not stand the sheer repulsiveness of the poison and its effects. Some ran away when they discovered who had injected the poison because they could not believe he could do such a thing.

But one person has stayed around. They've been interested enough to dig down into the soil and start to analyse it.

They've promised to find a way to start flushing the poison away. They tried to convince the island that it wasn't the island itself that was at fault but the poison that had made it barren.

The island has gained hope in its potential and even started to grow things. Roots had started to sprout and there were signs that it could even bear fruit.

Because of this new life, one or two people have started to stay on the island and appreciate it. One person is even soon to sign a contract so they can live on the island forever.

But now there seems to be a crisis. The specialist digging and flushing out the poison has suddenly decided to go. Maybe they got infected by the poison. Maybe they couldn't cope with the rotten smell the poison had caused. Maybe they found a new project which is far more interesting and worthwhile.
The problem is it's too soon. They had only just started to scratch the surface. They haven't dug deep enough. However, they are not willing to stay and see the project through.
The poison hasn't gone. If the specialist leaves now, it will be left to fester, to spread again, and all the new life will be killed off.
But there was not enough for them, and now they are committed to a new project.
The person who wants to live on the island wants to take care of it and help it produce new life. But they don't understand enough about the poison to get rid of it and stop it from spreading again. They don't have the resources or the skill to flush the poison out.

The island itself is in a desperate state. No one can understand what it meant to the island to be explored and understood, to have the truth of its history revealed and believe it could bear a life of its own after all the years of barrenness. To be given hope that the poison could be flushed out.
But now that hope has gone. The belief that one day, all the poison would be completely flushed away and the island could survive has gone.

It is only a matter of time until the island is barren again, the signs of new life are destroyed, and the people living on it decide to leave. The island is dismayed at going back to how it was. It tries to think of ways to destroy itself quickly and easily rather than experiencing a slow, lingering destruction.
All that waste.
All that hope destroyed.
All that potential lost...

"There's an island in the middle of the sea, in the middle of nowhere, miles from anyone, miles from anything. Just one small, solitary island. Not many people know it is there. To those who know of its meaningless existence, it is too far away, unreachable...
No one will know the pain, the heartache, the loneliness or the battles that the island went through in its struggle to survive, its fight to exist and grow... ALL IN VAIN..."

MJA 1993
©AIMtogetbetter2024

At the age of thirty- nine, the cycles of addictive behaviour came to an end following three years of counselling with a specialist eating disorder service. I never discussed anything to do with my father with the counsellor, but she did help me realise how my dysfunctional behaviours never actually helped me achieve what I was looking for and always resulted in more isolation and rejection. I overcame my eating disorder, and I simply stopped all my other behaviours. I also met Peter during this time, who became my soul mate, and we married a month before my 40th birthday.

Over the next few years, I convinced myself that I had "learnt to manage my mental health". In reality, I developed "avoidance behaviours" – one of the many symptoms of unresolved complex PTSD. I built up even more walls of protection around myself. I avoided any situation, such as going to church, where I would meet with the type of woman who fed my emotional addiction in the past.

Although Peter and I made friends with others socially, I always kept my guard up and ensured that I never opened up to any women. In my work life, I was obsessive about professional boundaries; I did not have any work colleagues as friends. I never spoke about my father, never opened up about "problems", and rarely went out socially. On the few occasions I did, I did not stay for long, wouldn't drink a drop of alcohol and never let my guard down.

These measures stopped the cycles of behaviour and helped me rebuild my career.

I learnt to trust Peter, and I felt protected for the first time ever. He never doubted my experiences and was always on my side. He supported me to back away from my family, but every time I did, I was consumed with such guilt that I could not stay away for long. I found it difficult to explain to him that, although every time I was in contact with them, I came away feeling like shit, and it could take me days or weeks to recover emotionally, it was easier to live with this than with the burden of guilt that came from trying to stay away.

Despite the positive changes in other areas of my life, the feelings of disgust and repulsion I felt when in the same room as my father never changed. Being in his presence reminded me that his shit (the guilt, repulsion, revulsion, disgust and layers and layers of toxic shame) hadn't just covered me inside and out; it had become such a part of me it was intertwined in every fibre of my being, spirit, soul and body. I had *become* shit.

HIV of the Soul

The reason that HIV is such a threat to the human race is that, as a retrovirus, it isn't like other microorganisms that use their own resources to replicate themselves. Instead, HIV goes into the body and seeks out a specific white blood cell called a T4 cell, which plays a key part in fighting infections and protecting the body from intruders. Not only does HIV hijack this cell, but it penetrates it at its core, infiltrating its very being, going into the nucleus and changing its genetic material. From that moment on, everything changes. Every time the cell replicates, instead of replicating its own genetic material, it replicates the virus instead, ensuring that every time it divides, it produces more HIV particles. This process only has to take place in one single T4 cell for it to start a irreversible process that will spread secretly until every cell of the body, including every teardrop, is contaminated. As more HIV particles are produced, there are fewer T4 cells available to fight incoming infections, so the body can no longer protect itself. A battle ensues, and a war wages. With new drug therapies, the production of HIV particles can be slowed down and destroyed, but they can never be completely eliminated from the body. The drug therapies may manage to reduce the virus particles until they are "undetectable", but they remain in the body, lying dormant (sometimes for years), until something triggers them into being active. The process of slow, methodical destruction starts again.
This physical form of HIV was known to be one of the biggest threats to the existence of humans in the 1980s and '90s.

But there is another form that very few people are aware of; HIV of the soul...

It doesn't affect the body of the individual. Instead, it invades the very fabric of their mind, spirit and soul. Just as the physical form of HIV can slowly and steadily attack and destroy every cell of the body without being noticed, HIV of the soul can invade and destroy a victim without anyone on the outside noticing. Often, only the individual knows and recognises that the destructive force is spreading and polluting every fibre of their being – whilst onlookers are oblivious because their physical appearance remains unchanged. Outsiders may, of course, notice that something isn't right. They may observe the individual behaving in unusual ways but are likely to rationalise this with negative labels such as "attention seeking". They look at the symptoms rather than the underlying cause. They fail to recognise that the individual is, in fact, using basic survival strategies to stop themselves being destroyed.

Just as physical HIV can be caused by the penetration of bodily fluids, HIV of the soul can be triggered by a man penetrating an innocent girl. As his sperm infiltrates her body, every aspect of her soul is penetrated with this aggressive virus. His sperm will soon wash away from her body unnoticed, but the invisible infection has begun.

It takes hold of the cells of innocence, purity and self-identity. From that moment on, the mind, soul and spirit are polluted.

As she grows up, an internal battle for the soul is raging. During her formative years, she should be developing as her sense of self, identity, and inner beauty start to flourish. But instead, he has penetrated her. His virus is irreversibly merged with her; there is no separation between his spirit and hers. His inner DNA has infiltrated hers. Instead of thriving, she is merely surviving.

Sometimes, she finds the inner resources to fight and produce some healthy cells. There may even be times when she thinks she has flushed him out completely.

But just like physical HIV, there is no cure. She will only be in remission. Even if the virus seems undetectable for long periods of time, it is still there, lurking, spreading its roots like bindweed or invisible cancer, until it finds the right moment to strike back with a vengeance, rampaging through the soul with a destructive force that will eventually wipe out the host.

Today, I have been on a journey into the depths of my soul in search of a 16-year-old who got left for dead after a terrifying trauma. I have had to wade through layers of slime and crude oil to find her in the hidden depths. She is full of self-hatred, self-disgust, self-loathing. Every time she breathes, she is overwhelmed with the rotten stench of her own soul. Her spirit is crushed, suffocated by a dark shadow of hopelessness. She doesn't want anyone to come anywhere near her because she doesn't want to be responsible for spreading the infection to them. She knows they will be overcome with the stench of sewerage that she is drowning in. All she wants to do is die and go to hell – she would have no chance of being let into heaven, and if she was, she wouldn't go in because the foul, repugnant excrement which is her would pollute heaven itself.

She makes numerous attempts to kill herself. Outsiders diagnose this as depression, attention seeking, behaviour problems, and personality disorders. They try to tell her she is OK, beautiful, normal, and has everything to live for.

They don't see the invisible virus. After 13 years of being abused, infiltrated, and penetrated, there is not a single fibre of her mind, soul or spirit that hasn't been hijacked by the virus. Every cell of her identity has been taken over by the foul-smelling, disgusting, filthy stench of his lust. It is so intertwined into her identity, the only way to be rid of it is to be rid of her

What can be done for someone with end-stage HIV infection? You know there is no cure. You know that it's too late for treatment. You know that it's terminal. All you can hope for is good symptom relief to make the inevitable end more bearable. You try and ensure someone is there to hold their hand and reassure them, so no-one dies alone.

Is it the same for HIV of the soul? Is there any way of bringing her back from the valley of the shadow of death, or should everyone just accept that what that bastard did is irreversible, that there is no antidote for the poison he injected into her, and the best possible outcome would be to let her out of her suffering and help her go to a place of eternal peace?

MJA Nov 2011

PART II

The Bear

Chapter 11

The Journey To Healing Begins

In November 2021, having had no contact with mental health services for over ten years, I was “triggered” by the behaviour of a work colleague.

Previously, she had occasionally acted in ways that made me fall apart, sometimes for several days at a time. I was terrified of her, but whenever I tried to talk to her about her unprofessional behaviour, she was so skilled at "gaslighting", she was able to totally convince me that it was me, not her, that had the problem. She had the same effect on my managers; whenever I went to them for support, I was made to feel that my communication and people management skills were to blame, not her.

On this occasion, however, her bullying behaviour was so extreme that it sent me into crisis. I couldn't stop crying for days. I started making myself sick (for the first time in over ten years), struggled to contain the impulse to self-harm and was plagued with suicidal ideation.

I was overwhelmed and couldn't understand why or how the behaviour of this individual could have such a devastating impact on me.

Once again, I had to engage with mental health services. I was in touch with the crisis team at least once a day. During one of these calls,

I was still trying to make sense of my response to my colleague's behaviour when I heard myself saying, "Because her behaviour is so unpredictable, I am terrified of her, always walking on eggshells around her; just like my three-year-old, lying in bed in the dark, terrified, never knowing when the monster was going to strike again!"

In that moment of clarity, it all made sense.

Over the next few weeks, as I continued speaking to the crisis team, I felt understood for the first time. Instead of feeling judged and labelled when I spoke about the battles I was having not to self-harm, they responded with empathy and understanding. I was finally given a diagnosis of complex PTSD. With the diagnosis came indescribable relief. As I continued to speak to the crisis team, they helped me understand that my patterns of behaviour and my response to the unpredictable behaviour of my colleague all made total sense in light of my traumatic past.

Now that I had started to talk about my childhood without being misbelieved, I decided to engage with a counsellor. I thought I just needed a couple of sessions to work out coping mechanisms to prevent me from being triggered by my colleague in the future. But in that first session, she helped me realise that I needed more than a sticking plaster and that maybe this was my time, an opportunity to embark on a journey that could lead me to deep and genuine healing.

This has been the most difficult thing I have ever done. I have now been attending weekly sessions for three years. Although I can see how far I have come, the end is not yet in sight.

Any journey into the unknown is scary. Healing from trauma takes time, and it takes strength and bravery to be willing to face the past in order to heal, rewrite your memories, and compose a new ending to your story.

Chapter 12

The Bear

Towards the end of my first session with my counsellor, as we were making a verbal contract to have regular sessions, I warned her that in the past, I had always pushed the boundaries too far with my therapists; all of my past efforts to resolve my issues had resulted in people walking away, or with me ending up in hospital because of my self-injurious behaviours.

Her response took the wind out of my sails. She casually said it wouldn't be a problem, that she could set her own boundaries and protect both herself and me.

During the next week, I decided that she didn't understand what I was saying, so I wrote a long piece about a ferocious grizzly bear that could go on the rampage and do unthinkable damage if the door to its cage was opened.

At the beginning of my next session, I read it to her.

"A big fierce grizzly bear has been locked inside a cage with its arms and legs tethered in chains. It has spent years being doped up with tranquilisers to keep it safe inside its cage. On a few occasions, a zookeeper has expressed an interest in getting to know the bear, hoping it can be tamed in some way. But as soon as the door to the cage has been opened, the bear has gone wild. The only thing to do to stop it from destroying everyone and everything around is to shut the cage door and tranquilise the bear back into its stupor. All the zookeepers who have attempted to tame the bear have quickly given up and run away as soon as they have realised how out of control and ferocious it is."

MJA Nov 2021

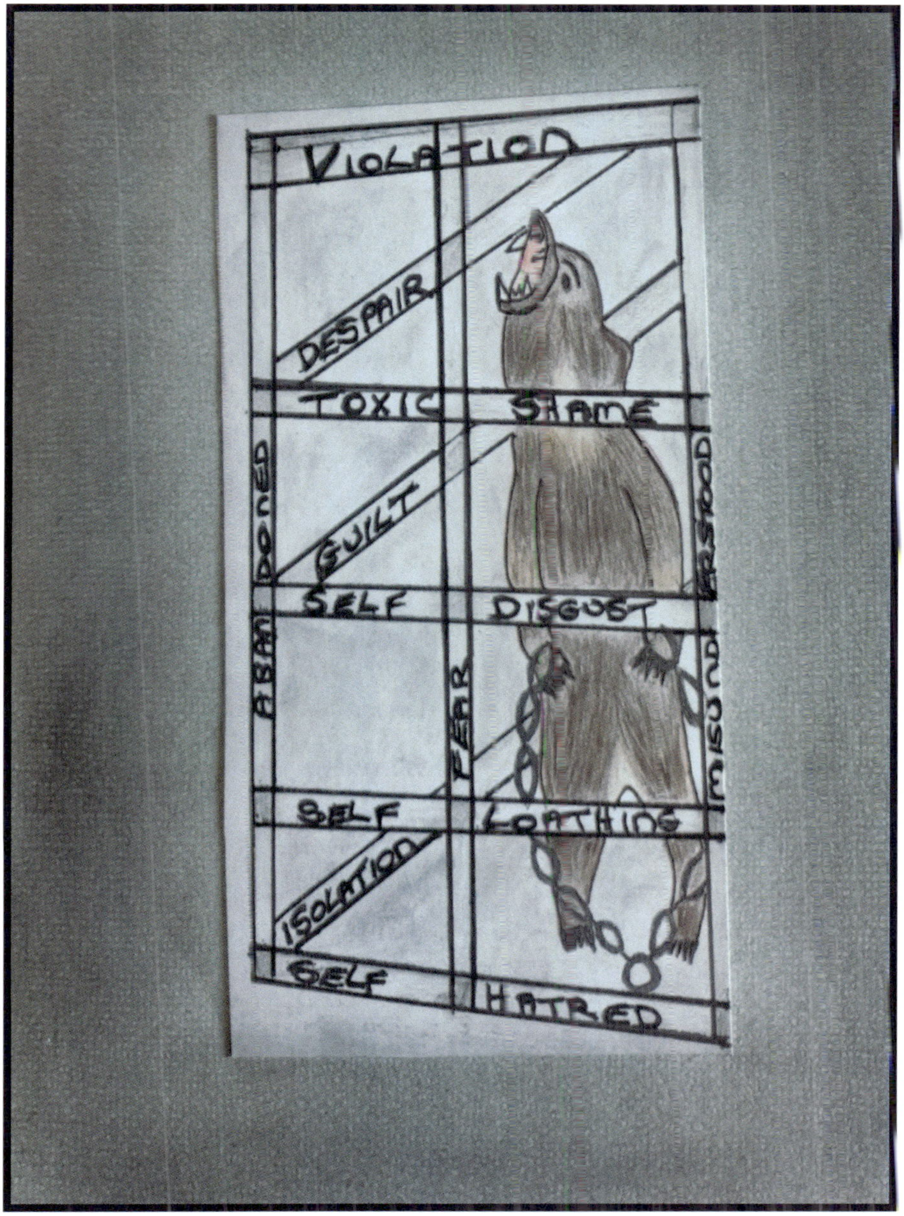
VIOLATION
DESPAIR
TOXIC
SHAME
GUILT
ABANDONED
MISUNDERSTOOD
SELF
DISGUST
FEAR
SELF
LOATHING
ISOLATION
SELF
HATRED

MJA Nov 2021

Once again, my counsellor's response was different from what I expected. She said that she understood why I felt the need to try and "warn her off" before we even started, given how many times people in the past had walked away. But she also said the grizzly was a "smoke screen". I asked her what she meant, and she told me a story....

Years ago, her young daughter insisted they take in a feral kitten. When they went to collect it, they got scratched all over as they tried to get it into the cage for the drive home. For the whole journey, it clung to the top of the cage, hanging upside-down, with its claws fully extended, hissing and meowing at the top of its voice. When they got home and opened the cage, the kitten ran behind the boiler and refused to come out. Its fur was matted with urine and faeces, and its stench was unimaginable, so they couldn't just leave it in that state. As they gave it a bath, it fought through the whole process, biting and scratching at every opportunity. Once the bath was over, the kitten ran back behind the boiler and stayed there for months. Every time they put down food or water, it lashed out, often drawing blood or "biting the hand that fed it". Although her daughter was understandably upset that it wasn't the cuddly companion she was hoping for, they did not give up on the kitten. My counsellor understood that it was lashing out to protect itself because it had been so traumatised and abused in the past. It couldn't trust anyone or anything because it was so frightened of getting hurt again.

Over the next few months, the frequency of lashing out reduced until it eventually stopped. After a bit more time, it started to poke its head out from behind the boiler, and when it thought no one was around, it would cautiously venture out, running straight back when a human came close.

After many more months, the kitten eventually realised that life outside of its self-imposed prison wasn't so bad. It grew up to be a splendid, brave, tenacious cat who enjoyed a good quality of life for many years!!

For the first two years of counselling, it felt like we spent a lot of time going round and round in circles. I would talk about how I was made of shit. She would tell me that, although she understood why I felt that way, it was the things that were done to me that caused me to feel like shit, not because I was made of it. I would get frustrated and argue, telling her she didn't understand or wasn't listening.

If she said something nice to me, I would retort that she was only being nice because I was paying her. And when she was really nice, or I felt genuine compassion for her, more times than not, I would shout at her to fuck off. This wasn't me playing games. I genuinely felt that the toxic shame, guilt, disgust and repulsiveness had seeped into and infected every fibre of my being, spirit, soul, and body see *"HIV of the Soul*" on p. 69

When I got frustrated and asked whether we should give up as it seemed like almost every session we were going around in the same circles, she would patiently explain that, although it seemed like going around in circles, it was a necessary part of the "deprogramming"; I had been so "brainwashed" by my family for so many years, we were actually going through a very slow process of challenging all of my dysfunctional thought patterns.

I spent most of those first two years feeling like that imprisoned grizzly, chained to the inside of its cage, doubting if it would ever be free.

It took a long, long time for me to realise that I wasn't *imprisoned* by the bars of that cage. Instead, the cage was *protecting* me. I could open it and walk out any time I was ready.

The "sumo suit" of my eight-year-old, the pig carcass enveloping my thirteen-year-old and the grizzly covering my adult were disguises which, although I detested, had kept people away. The reason I had spent years stuck in those cycles of addictive behaviours wasn't me "attention seeking" or playing some elaborate game. Instead, an innate survival mechanism was being triggered to push people away before they got close enough to see the real me. I needed to reject them before they could reject or hurt me. The very behaviours which had been labelled as "dysfunctional" by professionals were not dysfunctional at all; they were part of a complex but very successful survival strategy.

Of course, this strategy has one fundamental flaw. It may have helped me survive, but the very barriers or disguises I used to stop anyone from getting close enough to hurt me also stopped anyone from getting close enough to show love or genuine compassion.

For the first time, in my sessions with my counsellor, I experienced genuine compassion from someone who believed everything I told her. But instead of lapping up the love, I was resistant and rejected her kindness.

Over and over again, I would scream at her to fuck off when I desperately needed a hug. I was terrified that, just like all my previous experiences, if I allowed myself to open up, just at the point when I was most vulnerable, she would give up on me.

If I allowed myself to feel her acceptance and compassion, it would open up the chasm of emptiness and expose the black hole of neediness inside.

I was terrified that I would "need her too much", return to my emotionally addictive behaviours and sabotage the relationship.

Deep down, I knew that if I was going to allow love, compassion, positive energy, and healing in, it would mean removing the disguises and opening the door of the cage.

Repeatedly, just as I got to the point of letting myself experience love and acceptance, I would go into a blind panic and run straight back into the safety of my cage.

It is a frustratingly slow process. Not only does it require great tenacity on my part, but the people around me need the patience and understanding not to give up on me, to keep giving me hope when I despair, and to keep helping me hold on to the dream that one day, I will be able to come out of the cage, spread my wings, and fly.

Trapped Inside the Nightmare

Unlovable.
Untouchable.
Unacceptable.
Unreachable.
In the darkness.
Alone.

No one to turn to.
No one to talk to.
No one to reach out to.
No one there to rescue;
Trapped inside the nightmare,
On her own.

Nothing I can do
Will make this go away.
No words can explain
What I want to say.

Keeping the secret
Is more important than life itself;
Death seems a better option
Than carrying all this guilt.

No arms are strong enough
To reach across this void.
No love is deep enough
To fix what's been destroyed.

No amount of compassion,
Can heal this shattered heart.
Not even unlimited empathy,
Can mend what they ripped apart.

My reality was so unbelievable
I keep telling myself it was a lie.
My truth is so inconceivable
When I face it, I just want to die.

I don't know how to live with myself.
I feel so overwhelmed with disgust.
I don't know how else to see myself
Except as an object of lust.

I don't know how to live with this pain
It makes no difference when I cry
I know the only chance I have
It is to have you by my side.

But if you ask me how I'm feeling
I never know what to say;
I don't know why when I need you the most
I keep pushing you away.

But please, don't try to rewrite history
By telling me I was OK;
Because pretending that I was lovable
Would be like acting out in a play.

Telling me I was innocent
Is writing someone else's script,
So please don't tell me I was acceptable
When I know I was made of shit

Please, please don't try telling me
That I was not to blame,
As if that would somehow help
To take away some of this pain.

Please, please don't keep saying
That none of this was my fault
As if that, by some miracle,
It would remove all of this guilt.

I have no idea how to move forward
I feel so stuck inside my head,
I don't know how to accept the truth
Without wishing I was dead.

I know I need you to help me,
But instead, I push you away
How can I have hope in the future
When I don't know
How to get through today?

MJA Sept 2022

On reflection, I know I am not the only one who has spent most of my life walking around in a bear costume. I have come across many different kinds of bears in my life:

- There are the ferocious grizzlies that go around threatening to rip you to shreds. Only now am I truly beginning to understand that the more ferocious, aggressive, and threatening they seem, the more pain or trauma they need to protect themselves from

- Then there are the polar bears, which rarely come into contact with humans, spend their lives out in the cold, and grow a very, very thick coat of fur to protect themselves.
- Some brown bears dislike humans and can run fast and climb into trees to hide long before you know they are there. Although this makes them appear timid, do not be fooled; if you get too close or cause it to feel threatened, it will take a swipe at you and seriously injure you, possibly even killing you.
- Then there are the Pandas; docile, passive, and the least aggressive. We love their laid-back vibe, lying around as if they don't have a care in the world. But this is an illusion. They have long claws that can tear you apart and have a bite strong enough to break your bones. They rarely harm humans; if they do, it is usually unintentional, but you can never relax around them due to their unpredictability. Humans are drawn to Pandas by their cute and cuddly appearance. But this very thing that attracts us to them has made them victims hunted by predators to near extinction, making them an endangered species.
- Finally, there is Pooh Bear, the lovable character who is surrounded by friends with varying disabilities, from ADHD to chronic depression. Pooh seems to attract them all because he accepts them, regularly checks in on them and is happy to hang out with them, regardless of their mood or whether they are having a good or bad day. Although he is popular, he also has a compulsive eating disorder, and his need for a constant supply of sweet food can sometimes put his friendships and his safety in jeopardy. Feeding his addictive cravings comes before everyone and everything else.

I have spoken to many bears trapped in cages, most of them imprisoned by others' actions. Some will not even admit to themselves that they are in a cage or let themselves believe there is a world of freedom outside of its walls. Their denial is their security.

Others know that they are in the cage and know there is a door to freedom but are too safe in their prison to do anything about it, safe in the knowledge that the very walls that keep them in are, at the same time, keeping predators out.

There are also the bears who, when I have spoken about the journey that I am taking towards freedom, tell me they are too frightened—not of the freedom but of the process needed to get there. They are too frightened to face their demons in order to overcome them. They are too frightened to revisit their trauma so they can heal from it. To take off their disguise, they would expose their vulnerability—a risk they just aren't prepared to take.

Chapter 13

What Is Authentic Healing?

What is the relevance of the bear, and why is it essential that I recognise it as an elaborate disguise which I will, at some point, have to take off? Why can't I experience wholeness if I stay inside my self-imposed cage?

Every mystic I have read about, no matter what form of religion or spirituality they follow, has been through an experience described by many authors as "the dark night of the soul" (see recommended reading on p.214). This usually involves a personal crisis, making them question everything they thought they knew about themselves, their lives, relationships and values. This time of darkness or "unknowing" may last months or even years. When the person eventually comes out the other side, they are an entirely different version of who they used to be; the *authentic* version.

But this process isn't just for spiritual journeys. It is necessary for anyone who longs for deep and lasting healing from their past.

If your body is ravaged by an infection which, if left untreated, could threaten your very existence, the doctor treating you may find it impossible to administer the necessary treatment if you are wearing a metal suit of armour! You can't “heal” a disguise.

You will never discover your authentic self while you are pretending to be someone you are not.

The very best description of why this process is necessary is from a non-religious book called "Undefended Love" by Paris and Lyons (2022):

"To reach the unveiled part of ourselves that is deep enough to express the most profound and untamed aspects of our being means learning how to love and be loved without defences and obstructions. It means cultivating the capacity to be emotionally present even when we feel exposed or vulnerable, learning to relinquish the many strategies we have employed to feel safe and in control, and finding the courage to love without guarantees or requirements. By developing the capacity for intimacy in this way, we discover love as an abiding presence in the emotional centre of our being and heart. From then on, we will never again feel emotionally disconnected, incomplete, or unloved...

Most of us have defended and protected ourselves for so many years that we have lost direct access to our hearts; we do not know how to love unguardedly. . .

When we open our hearts to the wonder of the journey and search through the pain for the truth of our experience, we begin to glimpse a new light that will guide us deeper into ourselves, below our insecurities and the broken dreams of our lives. There, we will meet our whole, undamaged, and pristine essential selves. This is the promise of undefended intimacy. This is the satisfaction of the longing to love and be loved, directly, immediately, and without restriction."

Deep Sea Diving

There's a place that's deep inside of me
That I have never known;
A place I've always denied exists,
Too horrific for me to own.

A place that words cannot describe,
That no one else can know;
A place that cannot be survived,
Too distant for anyone to go.

Too dangerous to be explored,
Too dark for eyes to see,
Too far away for arms to reach,
Too disturbing to be believed.

Too unknown for minds to understand,
Too painful for a body to bare,
Drowning in emotions that can't be expressed,
And screams too loud for ears to hear.

And yet I'm being told that I must go
And uncover that place of pain,
To travel to its hidden depths
And unveil its horrors again.

To go back to the place, no one else can go,
And rescue the children that died;
To sink back down to those hidden depths
So that they can be revived.

So, I've decided to take the plunge,
To go through the scary darkness,
To leave behind all the things that feel safe
And sink to the very depths

But as soon as I jump, I stop hearing Your voice;
I'm full of panic and fear
How come now, when I need You the most
You've completely disappeared?

As I fall, I can't help feeling that I've made a mistake,
That You've done a runner and gone
As I sink further towards the lifeless seabed
I long to be held in Your arms.

As I lie in the darkness, I wonder why
There are times I feel you close when I pray,
But I can never find You when I need you the most;
When I'm in pain, you run away.

You tell me that when I'm hurting the most
You are sharing my grief and pain;
You hear every cry and silent scream,
You understand my shame.

As I fall to the bottom, I start to feel
The security of being caught in your arms;
As I learn to depend completely on You,
I find peace in the raging storm.

In the place of abandonment and despair
Your love starts to penetrate through,
As I live through this horror, you start to reveal
A "me" I never knew.

I find in the process of losing all that I have,
You give me back more than I need;
As I give up control of who I think I was
You're rebuilding a brand new me.

As I go through the place that's overwhelmingly dark
Your light starts shining in;
As I let Spirit search my inner parts,
I discover treasures buried deep within.

In this place of deepest pain
I'm discovering a deeper joy,
As I face the things that made me die inside,
I've found my spirit that can't be destroyed.

Although this place is full of trauma and pain,
There's nowhere else I'd rather be;
I never want to lose the mysterious love
That I've found in the depths of this sea.

MJA Mar 2022

Chapter 14

Authentic Healing In The Bible

In this chapter, I will describe a number of stories from the Bible that describe authentic healing. Even if you belong to a different religion or none at all, I hope you will gain something from my poetry and find healing and inspiration. But if, for whatever reason, you can't read this bit, feel free to move on to Part III.

The Story of Hosea and Gomer

Hosea was a prophet – someone who apparently heard directly from God and then told people what God was saying.

God instructed Hosea to marry a prostitute called Gomer. Hosea did what he was told, even though he knew his new wife would continue to be unfaithful. Now, the way we might expect the story to go is that, after years of showering his love onto her and not giving up on her, Gomer found some healing and started to love Hosea back. But no, she stayed with Hosea long enough to have 3 children "born out of prostitution" and then left them and travelled to another land so she could enjoy the expensive wine, food and clothes that her sex work bought her. Hosea did not stop her from leaving - he let her go because God had reassured him that "I will build a wall around her, shutting off her paths; she will pursue her lovers but will not find them; then she will say 'let me return to my husband, for it was better for me then than now.'"

Gomer soon realised that her old lifestyle and all the material goods that came with it were no longer satisfying her. God instructed Hosea to go and find her, which he did. But instead of taking her back home, he took her into the desert. In that desolate place, free of any distractions, Hosea showered love onto Gomer until she was able to love him back:

"I will bring her into the wilderness and speak tenderly to her to reconcile her to me; I will make the valley of trouble a door of hope; she will sing there and lie down in safety. I will betroth her to me in righteousness, justice, loving-kindness, loyalty, compassion and stability. Then, she will know....and respond with loving faithfulness."

Hosea chapter 2

Gomer's song

What is this? And who am I
That this man of God should love me?
I've become untouchable, and I'm filled with shame,
I'm completely unlovable – why can't he see?

I have run away to distant lands
And searched for love elsewhere;
I have intentionally done such terrible things,
Pushing away anyone who cares.

Seeking to meet my unmet needs
My passions spiralled out of control;
Consumed with guilt in my search for love,
I've travelled paths that no one should follow.

Yet now, I find I'm being pursued
By the one I hurt the most;
He has sacrificed all, left his whole life behind
In order to seek me out.

Why has he done it? What does he see?
Why give up his life to search out me?
Why not disown me like all the rest?
Why won't he leave me be?

Now that he's found me, there's nowhere to hide;
He sees all that I've done wrong,
And yet he says he wants to try again
And his love for me is still strong.

What kind of love is this,
That is determined not to give in?
A love that remains despite what I've done,
And sees through all of my sins?

A love that stays faithful after I have given up,
A love that won't give up on me.
A love that isn't tainted by who I've become,
And continues to believe in me?

How do I respond to such a love
When I've even rejected myself?
I am not worthy to even touch this man of God,
Yet he pursues me and wants to stay close.

He says he has come to take me away,
And that he wants to take me back home;
But before he restores me to my rightful place
He wants us to be alone.

He leads me along an unknown path,
To a place that is totally barren,
And there he begins to reveal his true love
Until I can trust him again.

His love for me has never changed
It was me that misunderstood;
Because no other love could reach inside
I never believed that he could.

In this desert, I'm being transformed
And I'm starting to understand;
As he reveals to me his unconditional love
It's creating an unbreakable bond.

This compassion is breaking down my defensive walls
To reveal what's really inside;
I'm discovering this love will never give up
And I no longer need to hide.

As this acceptance begins to dissolve my pain
And reveal the real me,
I begin to value who I really am
And discover my inner beauty.

His approval has uncovered a person of worth
Who no one has ever seen;
It gives me permission to be myself,
A "me" I've never been.

His arms have stopped me from running away
And allowed me to enjoy being held;
They have taken away my heart of stone
And turned it into gold.

There's also another change taking place
That I'm beginning to discern;
This love has somehow changed my desires
So I can love him in return.

I no longer want to pursue my lusts
And do the things I did,
I do not desire what once satisfied;
I just want him instead.

Could it be that this love provides
What others' attention has lacked?
The power to respond in an appropriate way
And be able to love others back?

Oh, how my heart is singing now,
Because my soul is free;
I can learn to live and love again,
Not afraid to reveal the real me.

I know I will never be pushed away,
However, I act or behave;
I don't need my defences; there's no need to pretend;
I've discovered unconditional love.

Oh, how my heart is loving now
The way it should always have done;
From this day on, things are going to change;
My life has just begun!

MJA 25.5.2003

The Religious Leader and the Tax Collector

In Luke chapter 18, Jesus told a story.

Two men went to the temple to pray. One was a religious leader, and one was a tax collector (two thousand years later, it's not difficult to understand why tax collectors were feared and hated. They were Government representatives with a job to do, but they were all corrupt, forcing people in poverty to pay more than they could afford in order to line their own pockets!!) The religious leader prayed loudly in front of other people, in a display of self-righteousness designed to boost his own ego: "Thank you, God, that I am not like other men; I am not like those that commit fraud, the liars, the cheats – or even like this tax collector!! I am good, I am honest, I pray to you often, and I put money in the Temple collection box!"

The tax collector, however, stood on his own with his head down, too ashamed to look up. He thumped his chest in distress as he cried, "God have mercy on me, for I am such a bad person!"

Jesus made it clear that it was the tax collector, authentic in his brokenness, not the religious leader, who had a true relationship with God.

The Woman at the Well

In John chapter 4, there is a story of Jesus having an encounter with a woman who was stuck in a cycle of behaviours that others disapproved of.

She was a Samaritan (a race deemed as "untouchable" by the more dominant religious community), she had been divorced 5 times and was now "living in sin" with a man she wasn't married to.

She had gone to get water from the well and had chosen a time of day when she thought she would not have to meet anyone – we could probably read into this that her shame about herself and her life choices had led to social anxiety and avoidance.

Jesus was sat alone by the well. As she drew water, He asked her for a drink. She was shocked – here was a man, a very religious man, a Jew, speaking to her, a woman, a Samaritan and an outcast. Perhaps He was mistaken? Just to be sure, the first thing she said to Him was to make it clear that she was a Samaritan. For some reason, this didn't put Him off, so she tried to go along with the bizarre conversation that followed. He was talking to her about giving her some magical water that would quench her thirst forever when He didn't even have a pitcher to draw any water out of the well! He then went on to say something that sent her into full-scale panic; He asked if He could meet her husband. Suddenly, she was vulnerable, and the conversation was going in a direction she didn't want it to go. She responded in a way that maintained as much dignity as possible: "I haven't got a husband!" This wasn't a lie. But it wasn't telling the honest truth.

So, how did Jesus respond? Did He go along with her attempt to save face? No. Instead, He replied, "You're right about that – you've had five husbands, and the man you're living with isn't your husband either!!" In that one response, He tore down her attempts to save face and exposed her for who she really was.

Why did He do this? Had He purposely reeled her into a conversation just so He could humiliate her, the way many emotional abusers gaslight their victims?

No. The truth was, in fact, the complete opposite. Jesus knew the only way to help this woman out of her cycles of rejection was through authentic healing. He knew how desperately she needed to feel genuine love and acceptance, but she was trying to hide who she really was because of her desperate need for approval. If He allowed her to keep those barriers up, His approval of her would be based on false pretenses. He had to rip down her masks, reveal the true state of her heart and then show her that He accepted her in that vulnerable, broken, rejected state.

Once her defences were down, He went on to tell her things that changed her life forever. He told her that she, a broken, sinful, rejected female, was just as entitled to worship God as the most respectable, male, Jewish leader: "For a time is coming, and in fact is already here when true worshippers will worship the Father in spirit and in truth (reality).

He was telling her that God wasn't interested in all the outer displays of religion and acceptability. He wanted people to approach God in the truth of who they really are, with no barriers or defences or pretence. Our acceptance is not based on our outer characteristics, background, gender, race, religion or behaviour. Our access to true love is through an honest connection to the Spirit. Anyone and everyone who is willing to have their ego and sense of "respectableness" stripped away and have their true identity exposed will have access to the source of grace, love, light and healing. They will experience true intimacy and authentic healing.

One of the Greek words translated as worship is proskuneo, which is derived from 2 root words; pros, which means "to lean towards", and kuneo, which means “to kiss”. This suggests that “worship” is not what most people do when they go to their temple or place of worship with a group of others, but instead, is an act of intimacy (Graham Kendrick, 1984).

Some may experience it by watching a sunset, being next to the sea, or hearing birds sing. Others find it through meditation or contemplation. Some may find it in silence. Others may find it through playing or listening to gentle music. Others may find it through poetry or creativity.

Whatever happened in that moment of enlightenment, the woman went back into her village as a totally transformed woman. She hadn’t had to “pray a sinner’s prayer” or perform any other kind of religious rite of passage that many Christians would say was necessary in order to be "saved". What had truly transformed this woman was understanding, in the core of her being, that she was just as worthy of being loved and accepted as anyone else. She had discovered the true meaning of grace.

Like a Bird Without a Song

Like a bird without a song,
Like a flower without its bloom,
Like a cloud without the sun
This is my life
When I'm distant from You.

Why is it that when I need you the most
You seem so far away?
Could it be that when You get close
I'm frightened you'll see the real me?

Is it me who puts up the walls
When I'm vulnerable and afraid?
Scared that when you see what's inside
You'll push me far away?

Are the things inside of me really so wrong
That they surpass Your desire to forgive?
Are my internal desires really so strong
They exceed the boundaries of Your unconditional love?

I never intended to cause you pain,
Or to make you hurt;
Can a heart that desires to please you so much
Also, be filled with such dirt?

I can't keep denying who I really am,
I'm exhausted from trying to change,
I don't have the energy to keep beating myself up
Or keep trying to hide my shame.

But can I really dare to believe
That in the past, I've got it so wrong?
If I'm honest and show you who I really am
Will your love for me remain strong?

Could it be that You see things differently
That you understand the things that took place?
That the events that have made me feel untouchable
Can be covered by Your grace?

"As far as the East is from the West
So great is your love for me!"
On this great truth, I will put my trust
And believe it will set my heart free!

Like a bird without a song,
Like a flower without its bloom,
Like a cloud without the Sun;
This is my life
When I'm distant from you.

MJA May 2003

The Woman with the Alabaster Jar

In Luke chapter 7, Jesus had been invited to the house of a religious man. Here was a group of men sitting around eating, drinking and chatting. Suddenly, they were interrupted by an uninvited guest – a prostitute. She burst in with a jar of very expensive perfume in her hands and threw herself at Jesus' feet. She was sobbing so much she was wetting Jesus' feet with her tears, so she dried them with her hair. She then broke open the jar of perfume and poured it over His feet.

The man hosting the evening was very put out by the interruption: "*If this man were a real prophet, He would know what sort of woman this is who is touching Him—she is a notorious sinner, an outcast, devoted to sin.*"

Jesus responded to him by saying that what this woman was doing was far more acceptable to Him than the show of outward piousness that the host and his guests were trying to display. He went on *to say, "She who sins much loves much.*" In other words, the more shame a person is carrying, the more they appreciate grace (unconditional acceptance). The more you realise you can't do anything to cover up your bad life choices, and the more broken you are, the deeper you will experience authentic healing.

The Fragrance of Brokenness

Like the woman with the alabaster jar
I pour myself out at Your feet;
I don't understand what it is about You,
But I've never felt this way before.

People around me are quick to condemn,
They don't understand what I'm doing;
They've seen my behaviour and judged my sin,
But they fail to see all the pain that's within.

Even I don't understand the things that I do,
Why I'm trapped into doing things that I hate,
Why I'm constantly tipping more disgust and shame
Onto the slag pile I've come to believe is me.

And yet, when I come near to You
I always feel very strange,
Because I know you see all the things
That have consumed me with guilt and shame.

Yet somehow, you look through them
And can see the real me,
You know that still buried deep within
Is the person of value You created me to be.

As I come before You and fall at Your feet,
There is something I must do;
Although I feel vulnerable and afraid,
It feels so different when I'm with You.

It seems such a stupid thing to do,
To want to be close to Someone like You;
What if You reject me or say I'm not good enough?
What will I have left if I give You all that I have?

Whenever I've felt loved before,
I've ended up being abused.
In the past, when I've given all my love and trust,
It's been repaid with more hurt and disgust.

But despite the fears, I know this can't wait;
I have to take the risk, and I fall at Your feet.
Like the woman with the alabaster jar,
I break myself open and begin to pour.

All that I am, I pour out at Your feet,
I despise it so much there's nothing I want to keep;
The sin, the guilt, the disgust, the shame,
The anger, the hatred and all of my pain,

The loneliness of being so misunderstood,
The isolation and violation of innocence lost,
My hopes, my fears, my shattered dreams.
The despair when I think of what could have been,

All that I am and wish I could be,
I pour it all out...I give You all of me....
As I give You everything and wash Your feet with my hair,
As I break myself open and pour out all my tears,

As I give You my pain and all the regrets of my life,
Into the depths of my darkness penetrates a shaft of light.
Between my cries, I hear You calling my name,
As You stroke my hair, I know You understand my shame.

THE BEAR, THE BULL AND THE BUTTERFLY

I dare to look up and through my hazy tears,
I see a face of compassion, eyes of acceptance and love.
I've never experienced anything like this before;
As I fall into Your arms, relief replaces all the fear.

Instead of rejecting my offering
Which was full of all the things I hate,
You have taken it, and in a way that I can't comprehend,
You have transformed it into a beautiful fragrance.

As I find security resting in Your arms
And in being held,
You take away my heart of stone,
And replace it with pure gold.

I've never known the acceptance I'm feeling in this place with You,
Or the safety of trusting a love that is pure;
Now I know that I can begin to hope and dream
That my heart and my life can be restored.

I've never known a place like this before,
Where intimacy springs from such sacrifice;
I never want to be without this fragrant love
That's flowing from my broken alabaster jar.

MJA April 1998.

Meeting Mary in the Place of the Dead

There are several different accounts of Easter Sunday in the Bible.

The account in John chapter 20 says that Mary had gone to the tomb to embalm Jesus' body when she discovered it was empty. She went to tell some of the men. They came to look for themselves, then went off with a plan to try and "fix" the situation.

But Mary remained alone at the tomb, crying and weeping. It was then that Jesus appeared to her.

Mark's account (Mark chapter 16) says, "*When Jesus rose early on the first day of the week, he appeared first to Mary Magdalene*."

So, why was Mary, a woman, the first person that Jesus appeared to? Why didn't He go to the men first?

The week before Jesus was killed, He had entered Jerusalem while crowds of people were cheering and shouting. After three years of telling his disciples that He was the Messiah, they were looking forward to Him being recognised as such – and, of course, them having a special status in His new empire. But instead, they had watched on helplessly as He went through a slow, degrading execution. All of their dreams were shattered. They were disillusioned and confused. So, they returned home and went back to the jobs and familiar life that they had before Jesus came along.

What about Mary? Why didn't she do the same? Why didn't she just go back to her old life?

We know that she had lived a life that made people look down on her and had suffered rejection as a result. And we know that instead of pretending to be something she wasn't, she allowed herself to be vulnerable and broken. As a result, her relationship with Jesus had totally transformed her; she had discovered her authentic self. She had found so much genuine love and acceptance that returning to her old, fake identity was inconceivable. It was better for her to remain in the place of the dead than go back to her old life.

The men had returned to "what they knew" and a life of familiarity. While they were off trying to "prove themselves" and problem-solve the issue of the missing body, Mary stood alone, broken and weeping. Now that she had experienced the true intimacy that comes from authentic healing, she could not go on without it. She was the first person to experience "resurrection life" on the first Easter Sunday morning because she depended on it the most.

The Promise of New Life

Humility instead of brokenness,
Healing instead of pain,
Wholeness transforming the emptiness,
Dignity overcoming the shame.

Adopted instead of isolated,
Child instead of orphan.
Love, healing the rejection,
Knowing I'm no longer alone.

Dreams replacing the nightmares,
Hope overcoming despair,
Light penetrating the darkness,
Courage instead of fear.

Cleansing of all the filthiness,
Acceptance instead of disgust,
Beauty rising out of the ashes,
Diamonds appearing out of the dust.

Gladness dissolving hopelessness,
Joy, instead of mourning,
Compassion replacing punishment,
Grace overpowering sin.

This is the promise of Easter
As Winter turns into Spring,
Dark nights will be replaced by the Summer,
"Where, oh death, is your sting?"

So, I will wait with patience.
Like Mary, when her hope had gone;
Believing in the promise
That new life will burst forth from this tomb.

MJA Easter 2022

MJA April 2022
©AIMtogetbetter2024

PART III

The Bull

Chapter 15
Changing My Mind

Undoing the brainwashing and psychological programming used by persistent abusers is a painstakingly slow process. Fortunately, our human brain has evolved with neuroplasticity – the ability to create new connections (neuropathways) and learn to think and respond differently. This transformation is essential if we are going to change our habitual thought patterns and behaviours. Still, it can only happen with a great deal of commitment, determination and conscious effort.

But before this process can even begin, you have to realise that you *have* been brainwashed, or at the very least, that your experiences have warped your view of reality. This requires someone to be brave enough to challenge your beliefs, assumptions, coping mechanisms and survival strategies with the strength and commitment to cope with the backlash of anger and denial that this will provoke. It is essential that this person has the skill and experience to know when to push and when to back off. Too much lenience and they will be colluding with your denial, delusional thinking and dysfunctional behaviour. But push too hard or at the wrong time, and you could become so overwhelmed that you implode or explode. They should not attempt to take away the coping and survival strategies you have relied on for years without first giving you new strategies; if a builder removes the scaffolding or internal props of an unstable building without first putting in new supporting walls, the structure could completely cave in!

Two and a half years into my counselling, although we had started to move forward, I still had times when I felt "stuck", where I couldn't change my mind over some of the most deeply rooted beliefs that I held about myself. And then I had a very dramatic, unexpected breakthrough.

On 24.6.24, Professor Gyozo Molnar gave a presentation entitled "*Imposter Syndrome*" at a postgraduate research conference that I attended at Worcester University.

He opened his talk by saying that, when he had first been asked to give this presentation, his first thoughts were, "*I can't give a talk on that"; "What do I know about this subject?"; "It's not something I have researched. I don't know enough!"; "There must be so many other people out there that could do a much better job than me"; Why have they asked me? "Is it really that obvious to all my colleagues in the university that I'm bluffing, and I don't really know what I'm talking about?" They must think I'm an imposter!"*

I considered it sheer brilliance to introduce the subject in this way, and I was mesmerised by the whole presentation!

Having introduced imposter syndrome, he spoke about Brene Brown's work on the power of stories, something I had never been made aware of before:

- Everyone has a story
- We form stories and stories form us
- Some stories enhance life, and others degrade it, so we need to be very careful about what stories we listen to and tell.
- You either walk inside your story and own it, or you stand outside your story and hustle for worthiness (Brene Brown 2012)

He went on to describe how Gabor Mate (2022) speaks about us all having two wolves inside us with opposing narratives: one for good and the other for evil. They compete with each other for food and attention. Whichever one you feed the most and spend the most time with will thrive; whichever one you ignore and stop feeding will get weak and eventually die. "The wolf we feed the most wins."

Professor Molnar then gave a summary of how to manage your imposter:

- Separate feelings from facts
- Accentuate the positives
- Develop a healthy response to failure
- Develop new scripts and stories
- Find a safe space for sharing your feelings
- Recognise, discuss and learn from your failures
- Celebrate successes
- Even when you fail at something, congratulate yourself on all the time and effort you have put in for having the courage to attempt it and CELEBRATE THE SUCCESSES YOU HAD ON THE WAY TO YOUR FAILURE!!!
- Be mindful of the stories you tell and the stories you are told
- Recognise your unique contribution to changing others' scripts and your own.

This was followed up by a presentation given by Trudie Holland entitled "*The Imposter Syndrome Gremlin*", who added some thoughts of her own on how to deal with your imposter:

- Visualise your negative gremlin/imposter and get to recognise them – what they sound like, the things they say, what their favourite phrases are
- When you hear your gremlin, start an argument with it
- If necessary, get a trusted friend to join the argument if you feel your gremlin is stronger than you
- *Start to rewrite the script and change how your story is going to end. You can only do this by facing and accepting it.*

The last point had a profound impact on me. It has taken me until the age of 58 to truly own my story rather than pretending it never happened, as I had been so programmed into believing that I had made it all up.

My counsellor often suggests, when I am reliving the horrific memories, that "I can change the ending", and we are currently going through a process of visualisation to change the endings of those memories and rescue the fragmented parts of me that have been abandoned for so long.

As soon as Trudie spoke about "visualising your gremlin," the first thing that came into my head was Ozzy, the mechanical bull built for the Commonwealth Games in Birmingham (UK), now homed inside the Bullring station!

My first thought when I saw this image was that this isn't just some little imp sitting on my shoulder but a gigantic, domineering, seemingly overpowering beast that makes me freeze in fear when it starts snorting and letting off steam. I cannot dare upset it or stand up against it, or it will charge, trample all over me, and possibly, completely destroy me.

My next thought was, *"The main thing that comes out of a bull is bullshit"*.

My next, most significant thought was that for all its bravado, it is fake, designed to instill fear, intimidation, and trepidation. IT IS *NOT* REAL. It is stuck in space and time. All I have to do is move away. It can't follow me, chase me, or trample me down. I can simply walk away and write a new ending to my story…

Photo taken by MJA, August 2022.

The Bull and the Butterfly.

Please note that throughout my story, the bull is referred to as a "she". This has troubled my cognitive, sensible brain and may trouble yours. All I can say is that I have recently discovered pragmatism – the philosophy of "do what works and change the rules if they are not working for you". I just know that the bull has to be a bull, not a cow. But it also has to be a "she"; it's the only thing that works for me. So, please put your thinking brain aside and travel with me on my journey to change the ending to my story………

Once upon a time, there was a little girl.
She didn't live in a normal family like other little girls.
Instead, she lived with a very large, very ugly, big, fat Mother Bull.

Mother Bull told her all sorts of lies, but the little girl didn't know they were lies - she believed everything Mother Bull told her. "You are so fat - just like me!"; "No one will love you because you are so fat!"; "No one will want to marry you until you get thin!"; "You will never get thin because you are my offspring - you have inherited my genes so you will always be a big, fat cow, just like me!"; "There's no point in doing ballet lessons or sports like your friends - you will never be good at them because you are so fat!"; "Just because you have done well in exams, don't you go thinking you can go to university or get a better job than me, as you will always be a failure because you are my daughter!"; "If your friends don't like you, it's because you are fat - you just need to go on another diet, and it will all work out!"

All the little girl wanted was to be loved and accepted by Mother Bull, so she was always very careful to do exactly what the beast told her to do. She made sure she was a very good, obedient child because if she ever disobeyed, Mother Bull would start snorting and stomping its foot on the ground, blowing out steam and frightening her into thinking it would reject her – or even worse, trample all over her, or toss her away with those big, scary horns. Although she never felt loved by Mother Bull, it was all she had, and maybe, just maybe, if she tried hard enough, she would finally gain the love and affection she always craved. She waited and waited and tried and tried, but nothing ever changed.

As the little girl grew into a teenager, Mother Bull became even more relentless in the endless criticism and onslaught of negativity, yet all the time telling her it was because she loved her and wanted the best for her.
The girl would do anything, anything, just to be loved and accepted. She tried so hard, she achieved the highest grades in her exams,

she starved herself and made herself sick, but even then, she never got good enough or thin enough to meet Mother Bull's approval or feel loved or accepted. Deep down, she knew her efforts were a waste of time and that she would always be a failure. She would never fit in; she would always be unlovable and unacceptable. When she was thirteen, she once told Mother Bull she wanted to kill herself and die, but Mother Bull got angry and started snorting and blowing steam out of her nose, telling the girl she was talking rubbish, and she was only saying this for attention. Mother Bull made her pray for forgiveness for being so bad and saying such terrible lies. After praying together that God would forgive her, Mother Bull stated that tomorrow, they would start another diet because all her problems would go away if she wasn't so fat.

The strange thing is that the girl still loved Mother Bull and didn't get angry or blame her because she knew a secret.......
The bull was not behaving in this way because it was evil. In fact, she never used to be a bull. She was once a beautiful, intelligent, and attractive young lady, the kindest, most caring young lady on earth. She had been brought up in an orphanage, so she had no idea what true love really felt like, yet she still managed to be kind and caring to others.

One day, she met a handsome prince. He promised her the world. She fell in love with him, and they got married.

Everyone loved the prince. The prince talked to people about God and convinced them he was very much like God. He was a good, upstanding, charismatic man who drew the crowds as he taught them how they could be as good and Godlike as him.
Everyone who met him believed he was truly a man of God, and many followed his teachings.
But what no one realised, is that he was a fraud. He wasn't teaching people about the real Truth or about the loving, pure Spirit that is God. Instead, he made out that God was a man who

ruled people with fear, just like him. If people didn't follow all these rules (that, in reality, no human would ever be able to stick to), they would have to pray for forgiveness, follow rituals and become members of his church, or they would be banished to hell for eternity. His version of God made people follow the rules out of fear. His version of love and acceptance was based on total obedience and subservience. He made people feel sinful and guilty for fulfilling their basic physical needs. Hunger was turned into greed, and sexual attraction was turned into lust so he could make others feel so guilty and worthless that they would look to him for help and forgiveness. It was all about domination, control and meeting his needs. No one could question his beliefs – you could either believe his message, become a Christian and go to heaven or burn in hell for eternity.

So rather than being a genuine, worthy prince, he was really a sad, disempowered, inadequate man. He was an imposter. On the outside, he needed people to worship him and look up to him. On the outside, he appeared to be the most loving, spiritual man on earth. But behind closed doors, he was completely different. He controlled and dominated his princess, took away all her power, ridiculed her, grinding her sense of self down to powder, until eventually, her whole identity had changed, and she had turned from a graceful, beautiful, kind young woman into a fearful, clumsy, anxious bull.

The Imposter-Prince made her work hard to keep his house clean and raise his offspring, keeping up the appearance of being the perfect family while telling the princess that he loved her. Because the princess had never experienced true love, she had no idea this wasn't how a loving relationship was meant to be. She could only pass her bullish version of love onto her children because she didn't know there was another way.
But it wasn't just her that the Imposter-Prince treated this way. Behind his preaching, pretence and powerful presence, he was hiding a very, very dark secret...

The emotional and physical starvation that the little girl endured from Mother Bull was nothing compared to the terrible, bad, painful, nasty things the Imposter-Prince did to the little girl in secret, in the dark. It made her feel disgusting and repulsive and full of shame, and yet he told her he loved her while he did it.
As she grew up, she was made to feel it was all her fault. The Imposter-Prince had made her feel that she really was that fat, ugly, disgusting, clumsy, unlovable bull that Mother Bull had always told her she would grow up to be.

When she became an adult and met new people, some of them could see through the bull disguise and tried to tell her that she wasn't who she thought she was. Occasionally, she believed it, but not for very long.
The Imposter-Prince, Mother Bull and her sons didn't want anyone to see the truth of who the little girl really was because if they did, and she told them how she came to be wearing the disguise, they would come to see that the prince was really an imposter. And because the Imposter-Prince's sons were like him in so many ways, they made sure she was never able to tell her truth. If she ever tried, they would silence her. On many occasions, she was locked away in a tower where they convinced her, and everyone else, that she was mad and bad and making it all up....

Years passed. The Imposter-Prince and Mother Bull died.
And yet still, the little girl, now a grown woman, continued to hear the voice of Mother Bull in her head. And she was still carrying around the big, heavy, filthy, disgusting, repulsive, smelly bull disguise that she had come to believe was her.

She had lots of people around her who saw through the disguise and could see it wasn't hers to carry. They desperately wanted to help her take it off because they could see the beautiful, genuine soul that was stuck inside.

But she became filled with fear when she tried to push the bull disguise off. In the past, if she fought or resisted or tried to take it off, the Imposter-Prince and his sons would push it down and tie it on even tighter than before, so she would always come off far, far worse.
So even though the Imposter-Prince and Mother Bull were dead, and their sons now lived in far-off lands, when she tried to take off the disguise, she was overcome with panic; she could still hear Mother Bull snorting, letting off steam and threatening to trample all over her.

But then, one day, as if by magic, she realised.
Just like that.

The bull was not real.
It never was.
It was always a disguise, designed to intimidate, frighten, and silence her from telling her story and stop her from being her pure, loving, and lovable authentic self.

Everything they had taught her and made her believe was all "bull".

In that moment, she knew that she knew, that the bull could snort and stomp its hooves and let off steam all it liked. But if she moved away, it couldn't come after her because it didn't actually exist, apart from in her head. All she had to do was move far enough away so that she could no longer hear the taunts and the threats and the lies.

All of a sudden, she also knew that she knew that the more she chose to move away from the bull when it spoke to her, the easier it would be to throw off the heavy, disgusting bull costume that had restricted her for her whole life.

And in the same magical moment, she also realised that hovering on the opposite side of her from the bull was the most beautiful, delicate butterfly she had ever seen, quietly singing to her. She had never heard her sing before because the noise of the bull's stomping and steaming had always drowned the song out.
But now, when she moved far enough away from the bull and stopped in the silence and stillness, she heard the butterfly's song. It was the most beautiful, healing song she had ever heard, telling her that she, too, was a beautiful butterfly who could, whenever she wanted, spread her wings and fly towards the sun.

As she listened to the soothing song, she felt sad that she had spent so much time being kept in the dark, believing the bull, and being weighed down by the disguise, when all along she could have been feeling the lightness, exhilaration and warmth of flying towards the sun.

So, she went out into an open, safe space and threw off her disguise. She felt very vulnerable now that she had lost the protection that the bull had given her for all those years. But within that vulnerability, she had the security of knowing that, when trouble came, she could spread her wings, rise above, and fly towards the light.

And now, my friend, it is time for you to learn from my story.
Everyone has an imposter on their shoulder, telling them lies and making them doubt themselves. But on the other shoulder, there is a quiet, unassuming butterfly.
Yours is whispering your truth, but you will only hear if you turn away from the noise and the bull, quieten yourself, and listen.

The bull or the butterfly?
Which one will you listen to in times of self-doubt?
Which way will you turn in times of trouble?
Who will you choose to be as you journey through your life?

Will you be true to your own story and live as your authentic self
Or will you stay in the safety of the protective disguise,
frightened to challenge all the bull you've been told?

The bull or the butterfly?
If, at some time in the future, you are walking in the countryside,
And see a butterfly flutter by,
It will be me.
There to remind you:
If you listen to the right voice,
You, too, can spread your wings and fly.

MJA 30.6.24

No other single event since starting this journey has had such an immediate and profound effect on me. On that day, I recognised the bull for what it was; my mum's narrative, not my own. I visualised myself walking away from the bull without fear and started to play a new script in my head. I stopped beating myself up constantly. I stopped reacting with revulsion every time I saw my reflection. And I started to listen to the gentle, new song of the butterfly.

However, I need to be realistic here – just because I decided to walk away from the Bull doesn't mean I was suddenly "happy ever after". Letting go of the negative doesn't mean the positive instantaneously flooded in and took its place. Instead, I have been left with a vacuum, which, in many ways, is more difficult to live with than the familiar negativity. It is in those moments of emptiness that I listen to the songs of hope that the butterfly brings to me (see part v, page 191)

I hope, at some point, the vacuum will slowly be replaced with positive thoughts and emotions about myself.

Chapter 16

Changing My Mind About Me!

Enough

I was never going to be enough...

Never tall enough,
Never thin enough,
Never attractive enough,
Never feminine enough,
Never good enough,
Never clever enough,
Never successful enough.

After all these years, I've come to realise
That nothing I could ever do would make me acceptable in your eyes.
This was all about you, never about me;
I was taking the blame for all your unmet needs.

You could never truly love me because you never loved yourself,
Expecting me to succeed wherever you had failed.
To hide from your own insecurities , you pushed them onto me,
Never allowing me to be myself, or be who you could never be.

Blaming me for all the things that made you disempowered,
Taking control of my body and mind because you felt out of control of yours.
Holding me to ransom, making me pay the price,
Never giving me the freedom to live out my own life.

And now I am having to grieve the loss of wasting so much of my life,
Thinking about what could have been if I had been enough in your eyes.
I've had enough of pretending to be the person you could love;
I've had enough of acting out, trying to be someone that I'm not.

I've had enough of forcing myself, of driving myself into the ground,
I've had enough of the circles, and spinning round and round.
I've had enough of pushing my limits to the nth degree,
I've had enough of punishing myself when I don't succeed.

I've had enough of the disappointment, of feeling you disapprove,
I've had enough of the heartache, of never feeling loved by you.
It's time to stop beating myself up for the things I could never control,
I have to stop taking all the blame, I need to learn to let go.

I need to accept who I really am and let myself be me,
Embrace every facet of my true self in order to set myself free.
I need to have faith that I'm OK, allow myself to feel loved
I need to stop listening to all your lies, and believe that
I AM ENOUGH

MJA 19.3.23 (Mother's Day)

Letting Myself Be Me

I don't have to be ashamed of it,
I don't have to keep it buried,
I don't have to keep it a secret,
I don't have to pretend it isn't part of me,
I don't have to strive to be someone I'm not
In order to be accepted and acceptable.

Every time I tried to talk about it, I was forced to stop.
Every time I spoke about it, I was made out to be a liar.
Every time I tried to expose what they did
I was made to feel the guilty one, and they became the victims.

Every time I was in a room with him, I felt sick, I felt "gunged" and polluted.
I can't even put into words how I felt when he put his arms around me;
The stench, the filth,
Having to swallow down the compulsion to vomit.

And yet, I was expected to do just that.
To smile, to pretend, to swallow it all down;
Made to feel guilty when I couldn't swallow hard enough,
When I couldn't make my smile wide enough to keep up the pretense.

Somehow, it was my fault if I chose not to play along,
If my acting skills weren't good enough
Or I didn't have the emotional energy
To keep playing the 'happy families' game.

I was even made to believe that if I forgave him,
I wouldn't have those feelings.
So, I forgave and forgave and forgave every day.
But my prayers were not powerful enough to make it go away.

That made me feel more guilty, that it must be my fault;
The rest of my family can play along, so why can't I?
I am a disappointment.
If I can't fit in with my own family, where can I belong?

I can't change the way he makes me feel,
Yet, I am made to feel that I am to blame...

But now, for the first time ever, I have let people see the real me
Rather than the version I think they want me to be.
And I feel accepted in a way I have always longed for
But never known.

For the first time ever,
I am beginning to see that

IT'S OK TO BE ME!!
I don't have to be ashamed,
I don't have to keep it quiet,
I don't have to feel guilty for talking about it,
I don't have to hide it away, or keep my story a secret.
I don't have to pretend anymore.
I don't have to keep sweeping the broken pieces of me into the bin
I don't have to keep covering up those parts that have never been exposed
Because of the layers and layers of shame.
I don't need to hide the real me away.
I don't have to keep trying to be a more acceptable version of me.

I CAN BE ME!!
Without shame.
Without guilt.
Without hiding away.

I CAN DELIGHT IN BEING ME!!
In all my damaged glory.
My inner beauty
Enhanced by the ugly scars.

MJA 17.7.22

Chapter 17
Changing My Mind About My Body

Most of my dysfunctional / emotionally addictive behaviours revolved around my body. I internalised all of the shame, disgust, revulsion and repulsion because I could not direct it externally. When I cut deeply, it was usually across my lower abdomen, trying to somehow "cut out my womanhood". I spent almost 35 years starving myself, making myself violently sick or abusing laxatives. When I looked at photos of myself, I felt violent repulsion, disgust and hatred.

Over time, my counsellor helped me realise that, from the photos, it was apparent that the times when I was at my most obese were the times the abuse was most prolific. When I was having a reprieve from the abuse, I was slimmer. The fact that I hated my body so much was a form of protection. It gave me somewhere to store all those extreme emotions I could not express outwardly. My body saved my life!

To My Body

Thank you.

For the last 50 years I have hated you,
Felt nothing but disgust for you,
Been overwhelmed by shame and so repulsed by you
I have wanted to vomit every time
I have looked at you.

I have mistreated you,
Punished you,
Cut you to shreds,
Starved you,
Stuffed you full, then violently purged you.

But against all the odds
You survived.
You allowed me to blame you,
Project all my feelings onto you,
Because you knew....

I was so vulnerable, so defenseless,
So often forced into that space between life and death
That if I tried to fight back,
If I had placed the blame where it really belonged,
I would have been destroyed.

What you have done for me is nothing short of a miracle.
You are so very strong.
You have put into place survival strategies
That my conscious brain
Could never have conjured up.

You have experienced such terror,
Such fear, such pain.
Unimaginable horror, at times so excessive
You had to force my soul to detach itself from you
As you clung on to life by a thread.

I am in awe of you.
I am so grateful to you.

But now, after 50 years
Of living in high threat, fight or flight survival mode,
It is time for you to stand down....
The threat has gone.
It will never return.

I now have an army of true friends,
Who will look out for me,
Protect me,
Love and nurture me,
While I learn to look after myself.

It's time to rest.
It's time to heal.
I will do my best
To feed you, protect you,
And bring you to a place of optimum health.

I will no longer hold you responsible., none of it was your fault.
You can start to release the guilt, the shame
The disgust, the repulsion, the blame.
I don't want you to hold on to any of it;
You can let go of it all.

With help, as you relinquish it,
I will put it back where it belongs;
Hand it back to the people
Who should have carried this burden
All along.
From now on, with every breath,
With every heartbeat, with every moment and every step,
I will respect you.
I will be kind to you.
I will be forever grateful to you for bringing me this far.

And I will look forward with hope
As we embark on this new journey of discovery
Together.........

MJA 24.11.23

Chapter 18

Changing My Mind By Changing The Memories

The House of Horrors

There's a big, derelict house that hardly anyone knows is there. Not only is it located behind high walls with a gate firmly chained up with a padlock (for which no one seems to have a key), but the surrounding garden is so overgrown with trees, brambles, nettles, and holly bushes that people assume it's just a wild garden and have no idea there is a house inside.

No one has entered the house for years, and it is totally inaccessible. It really needs to be knocked down, gutted, and cleared away so that a new, fit-for-purpose house can be built on it. But the owner knows they can't clear the land and demolish the house because it has hidden secrets. Although most of the dust-covered items in the house are useless and just need dumping or burning, there are also hidden treasures that need saving first...

There are children trapped inside its rooms, frozen in time, with stories of inescapable torture. Some are imprisoned in rooms that would be accessible if the right person tried to find them, but others are buried deep in the basement, trapped behind thick doors that are firmly locked and bolted.

Eighteen months ago, the owner decided it was time to sort the house out, remove the valuable items to a safe place so the house can be knocked down and the land repurposed. She employed a specialist to try and gain access to the house. However, the owner had not predicted how challenging the job would be. Cutting off the padlock, taking off the chains tightly wrapped around the gate, and cutting a path through all the brambles to the front door has been far more demanding and time-consuming than the owner could have imagined. She has had to place trust in the specialist, especially when the path has taken some unexpected twists and turns. There have been numerous times when the owner has wanted to give up, leave the kids locked up in their dungeons with their screams echoing throughout eternity and walk away.

However, the owner has one or two friends who, although unable to enter the grounds of the house themselves, encouraged her to keep going because they see the potential in this land.

One of the reasons it has taken so long to even start this renovation is that when she has spoken of her plans in the past, some of her family members put up strong resistance. They worked tirelessly to stop the work going ahead. She has never fully understood why, but the most probable explanation is that if she successfully completes the work, it will expose the fact that they have not done the necessary work on their own properties, which are even more inaccessible than hers.

But now, the owner has a partner and a team of supporters encouraging her to stand up and fight to repossess what is rightfully hers. Her partner is employed as a security guard, ensuring that those family members who have, in the past, violently sabotaged the work (before it even got off the ground) don't come back.

Although the process of clearing a path to the front door has been slow, it has given time for the owner to realise that all of the overgrown bushes and brambles have served a purpose – they have actually offered the house protection from the elements and have, without a doubt, kept the intruders out. It has also given the owner time to re-familiarise herself with the layout of the house. As she had done so, she had to face the very, very painful reality of what happened to each of the children who remained trapped inside their torture chambers.

And now, the moment of finally opening the front door and stepping inside is closer than ever. The owner can even hear one of the children sobbing and crying out for help, desperate to be reached.

But now, this moment is finally here, and the door has been opened, instead of stepping inside, the owner stands frozen on the threshold.
She wants to run away, but she doesn't know why.
All the work of the last 15 months has been to get to this place and rescue the children. They are within reach. But for some reason, she wants to scream and swear at the specialist, who is standing beside her, and sack her!

Maybe the owner should never have started. Maybe she never believed the children could be freed and healed from their experiences after all this time. Maybe she should run back out and lock the gates firmly shut.

MJA 1.8.23

It's over a year since we entered the house of horrors for the first time, yet there are still rooms we haven't explored and children we haven't yet rescued.

Just clearing away the undergrowth and getting to the front door was a slow task because of all the emotions it brought up.

Each time we went back to the house, I knew it was time to rescue another part of me. The dungeons are located in different parts of the house. Some are in the basement, some on the first floor, and some in secret compartments you wouldn't know were there.

The first one we went to rescue was my eight-year-old, who was in a room on the first floor – she was the one I could hear crying as we opened the front door. As soon as we walked in, she ran into my counsellor's arms and sobbed her little heart out. But once we got her to the safehouse, she climbed into bed and hid herself under the duvet, refusing to come out. After a while, I realised it was because she knew I still didn't really like her. I was holding on to my resentment of her and still felt ashamed of her. Once I could let go of those feelings, she let me jump under the duvet and cuddle her. We were there for many more months before we eventually came out from under the duvet and started discovering the new life waiting for us outside.

My thirteen-year-old was hidden in a corner of the basement. It was so dark down there – and she had covered herself in sackcloth to make herself invisible. Unlike some younger ones, she wasn't waiting excitedly for someone to find her – she didn't want to be found. It took a lot of time before she was persuaded that she was worthy of being rescued and didn't deserve to spend the rest of eternity hidden away in the dark. When we got her to the safe house, she ran into a room, locked the door and switched off the light. I often went to check on her and heard her frightened voice, "Go away and leave me alone". For months, I stood outside the door, gently telling her I was sorry that I abandoned her, blamed her and hated her. I now understood that none of this was her fault, and she didn't deserve any of it. A few weeks ago, she finally opened the door and let me in. I have since been standing with her, holding her tightly in the dark until she feels ready to venture out.

To get to my fifteen-year-old, we had to go back down into the basement and find a secret trap door, then make our way down a flight of broken, rotting steps that led to a cellar that no one realised was there

– deep in the foundations of the house. Due to a problem with leaking pipes, the cellar was waist-deep in sewerage. My counsellor and I had to wade through the shit until we eventually found her, totally submerged. With my help, my counsellor scooped her in her arms and took her to our safe house, where we bathed her regularly in warm water; the shit didn't come off all in one go, as some of it had been stuck to her for so very long, and she had also ingested some of it. The process is still ongoing, but over time, with gentle encouragement from my counsellor, I have occasionally been able to take the warm, soft towel and wrap it around her myself.

With each rescue, we are visualising a different ending to each of the memories and changing the story.

We still haven't recovered all of them. It can be weeks, if not months, between each rescue. The process can be overwhelming. A very cathartic session, which makes me feel I am finally getting somewhere, may be followed by a number of seemingly "time-wasting" sessions, where I am back in my grizzly suit, closed off, zoned out or curled up in a "freeze" state. I find these times frustrating and often ask, "I feel stuck; am I *ev*er going to get out of this cage?" My counsellor reassures me that my brain is telling me I need a break from the exhaustion and overwhelm, and we will move on when I am ready….

The Treasure in the Tombs

I don't know how to go forward, but I know there's no going back.
I don't want her in my life, but I can't leave her behind.
I need to dissociate myself from her, but I can't be me without her.
I don't want her to be part of me, but I can't be whole without her.
I can't live with her, but I can't be alive without her.

How many times do I have to return
To this hopeless place of despair:
Fumbling around in the darkness,
Wishing I could disappear?

I keep thinking I'm moving forward,
That my path is becoming clear;
But whenever I get close to my 'promised land.'
I end up back in this valley of fear.

I know I can't go backwards,
Or return to the place I came from,
So, instead, I go around in circles,
Incapable of moving on.

Why do I keep ending up here,
Coming back again and again?
Non-existing in suspended animation
Inside a nightmare that never ends.

Some people say it's on purpose,
That I stay here in the place of the dead;
That I've got so used to drowning in terror
I'm too frightened to let myself live.

But there's something hidden within each tomb,
That I just can't leave behind.
I've tried so hard to forget them,
And put them out of my mind.

I've tried to travel to far-off lands,
To make a new life of my own.
But I'm compelled to return in order to reveal
The jewels, hidden behind each stone.

The treasure actually belonged to me,
Back at the beginning of time:
But I was raped and robbed and damaged beyond repair,
As they stole what was rightfully mine.

The damaged goods were hidden away,
In the hope that no one would notice.
Although, through the years, the world has moved on,
They are preserved in a vacuum that's timeless.

So, you see, I have to keep coming back
To reclaim the treasures they stole.
If I don't reclaim every missing piece,
I will never be able to feel whole.

Each time I return, it's to remove another stone,
To search every inch of that tomb
Until I find another missing piece:
A precious jewel to take home.

The process causes so much pain and fear,
As I enter those dungeons of terror,
But if I don't fight to set those captives free,
They'll remain lost and broken forever.

So, although it appears, I'm going round and round,
And it's all a waste of time,
Each time I return, I grow just a little bit stronger,
As I fight to reclaim what is mine.

I will not stop until I've claimed it all back,
And plundered every tomb;
Transplanting dormant seeds back to life,
Ensuring each trampled rose is revived.

One day, I'll be reunited
With every missing part.
My greatest reward, my best revenge,
It is to rebuild my shattered heart.

So, in these times of darkness,
When I'm consumed with despair and pain,
I will take courage and hold on to the hope
That I will see daylight again.

One day, I will leave this valley of death,
And never need to return.
So, I will hold on to life by clinging to the threads
That promise rainbows after the storm.

When that day comes, I'll be empowered by joy,
I will spread my wings and fly.
Instead of non-existing in the shadow of death
I'll be gliding across blue skies!

MJA 17.3.24

Chapter 19
A World Full Of Bull

Since recognising my own imposter bull, I have noticed just how many bulls there are bumping their way around in life. It is my impression that most of them have no insight into the fact that they are controlled by an imposter.

My parents' post-war generation was brought up in the "stiff upper lip" era, who never spoke about their abuse or trauma (these words didn't come into the English vocabulary until the 1980s). People showing outward displays of emotion were seen as "weak", especially men, and there was great shame associated with anyone who had a mental illness or learning disability – so much so that many of these people were locked away in institutions and never came back out. As a result, people have had to take on a mindset and persona where they have to be strong and show no weakness. Any appearance of vulnerability could trigger memories where others took advantage of this vulnerability, so it is necessary to put on a show of strength at all costs. As I have reflected on this, I have decided that those people with the hardest, most threatening and obnoxiously selfish "I don't care about anyone else" persona are probably the most hurt, who have had to put an unfathomable distance between themselves and their authentic, vulnerable, damaged self.

In my generation, as the media industry has grown and 24-hour access to radios, TVs and social media has been made available globally, and we are constantly being programmed with messages from a different type of imposter bull. You have to look a certain way and consume certain brands to be acceptable. As attractiveness became confused with glamour in the 1960s and 70s, the pressure to conform to a certain body shape became immense. The diet and fitness industry expanded as people's waistlines shrunk. At the same time, as music and sports industries became more commercialised, there was increased pressure to "follow" a certain genre of music or football team. As we became adults, there was increasing pressure to wear designer clothes or have an expensive brand of car. We were part of the "buy now, pay later" culture – if it feels good, do it; if you want it, buy it; if you crave it (food, sex, tobacco, drugs), have it now – worry about the consequences later. When it no longer meets your needs or expectations, discard it and move on to something else.

The more we have changed our behaviours, attitudes, beliefs, and values to "fit in," be accepted, and find a sense of belonging, the further disconnected we have become from our authentic selves. We are drowning in the relentless noise and clamour of the bulls around us. We don't know how and when to switch it off, so we are permanently submerged in it. We no longer have the opportunity to find the stillness and silence required to hear the song of the butterfly.

For the younger generation, it has become even worse. Instead of having to contend with just their own herd of bulls, the voice of "influencers" from around the world is being heard far louder than the voice of parents or teachers. It is now easier than ever to create a fake identity and photoshop your image, erasing the bits you don't like. It is cheaper than ever to pay to have surgery, either to permanently change your facial features or to cut out half your stomach so you get thin quickly and easily, rather than taking the time and self-discipline to lose weight the conventional way.

Not only has "fake news" become a daily reality so that we can't believe anything we read or hear (a phrase coined by one of the most fake humans on the planet), we can no longer believe what we see. The term "deep fake" is now often used when photos or videos appear on social media that have been edited so well that it is impossible for a "normal" person to tell that they are not real.

Perhaps the rise in mental health issues, depression and anxiety in recent years isn't just down to the trend in "self-diagnosis via Tic-Tok"; maybe it's because, deep down, there is something missing – the connection to our authentic self.

But the place where I have come across the most bulls is within the Christian church. So many people hiding behind their faith, striving to be someone they are not, in order to fit in and meet the criteria for finding approval from God and other members of their church. Perhaps the reason why, to outsiders, many Christians appear to be so "fake" is because it is their "false self" that has been "saved" when, in reality, our authentic self doesn't need to be saved, it needs to be discovered?

One of the main reasons I stopped going to any church service is because, regardless of what type of church is it (Baptist, Church of England, Charismatic), there is always someone at the front, telling you what to sing, praying on your behalf, and preaching at you to convince you what you should believe and how you should behave. These services are always so "busy" there is hardly ever any time given to sitting in silence and connecting with Spirit in an authentic way, allowing you to hear what you need to hear for yourself.

PART IV

The Journey

Chapter 20

The Journey

(Inspired by "Divine Beauty, The Invisible Embrace" by John O'Donoghue)

On the first day of the first module of my PhD, we were given a list of the skills and qualities required to be a successful postgraduate researcher. Our first assignment on the long path to becoming a researcher was to carry out a self-assessment, identify the areas where we had skill gaps, and create an action plan for developing those skills.

As it had been over 12 years since I completed my Master's, I already knew that I had a lot of catching up to do in relation to getting back into postgraduate study, especially with regard to the cognitive skills required for actually carrying out research and writing a thesis. It came as no surprise to me that I scored myself low in these areas.

What I wasn't expecting was how high I was able to score myself in the areas that, in my mind, are more about character than intellect—those attributes that come through "lessons in life" rather than from reading a textbook: enthusiasm, perseverance, integrity, responsibility, responsiveness to change, respect. As I worked my way through my self-assessment, something dawned on me like never before.

Nothing I have gone through has been wasted. Every day, every experience has been leading me to this threshold, preparing me for this next step in my journey.

I have spent so much of my time living in regret. I have felt I had failed in my career, never being able to hold a job down for more than a few years; every time I found something I enjoyed or gained a promotion, my mental health would let me down, and I would be forced to leave. I thought I'd had a lifelong "calling" to go to India, but on my third trip, I got "triggered", became very ill and was forced to return to the UK. I tried to continue in nursing, but I was too "burnt out" and felt I had nothing left in me to care, so I went into teaching. Whilst in that role, I gained a teaching qualification as well as completed an Open University degree in Health Promotion. This led me to a job in Public Health. I spent over £10,000 of my money, studying every weekend for over three years to gain my Master's in Public Health. But once again, I kept being "triggered" in that job. By the time I graduated with my MSc, I'd had to leave. Since then, whenever I look back, I have done so with self-annoyance; what a waste of time and money. Why did I ever think it would make a difference to my career?

I ended up getting a job in a nursing home because it was something I knew I could do; it would tide me over until I could decide which direction to go in next. But in that role, I flourished. I discovered that dementia care was "my true calling". Within months, I was promoted to the position of the Head of the Unit. I stayed for over 6 years, leading my team through the trauma of COVID and helping the home move from "Requires Improvement" to "Outstanding". There were many frustrations along the way, but since I have been promoted to my current role, I am grateful for every day I experienced in that job, because of the knowledge, experience, competence, confidence, communication and leadership skills it gave me.

Until now, I have looked back over my career with self-regret and extreme frustration with myself, wondering what I could have become if my parents had not done such a fantastic job in screwing me up.

But now, for the first time ever, I am seeing it from a completely different perspective. Every job, every job loss, every U-turn, every failure has all been in preparation for this moment. If I hadn't completed my Master's degree, I would not be able to embark on my PhD. If I hadn't had all the different jobs, I would not have

developed the breadth of skills and the depth of character needed for both my job and the study I am embarking on.
Until now, I have viewed my personal life in the same way, with regret, frustration and deep shame. I see all the times I have taken wrong turns, gone up blind alleys, got lost in a maze, got stuck on a roundabout, endlessly going round and round in seemingly pointless circles or ending up on the dodgems, clumsily bumping into things whilst getting absolutely nowhere. I get very cross with myself for wasting so much time. I think about where I have got to and where I seem to be heading and feel hopelessly jealous of those who appear to me to already be at their destination – those who seem to have "made it in life" and seem to be permanently in a much better place than me. But I also look at others who have driven themselves off a cliff or permanently parked up in a layby; sometimes, I look at them with compassion and think about how I could offer them a lift, but at other times, I look down on them judgmentally, as if I am somehow heading towards a better outcome than them. At other times, I race past people who have hit barriers, feeling arrogant and smug and sticking my fingers up at them as I race past.

But today, I realise that all that comparison with others is completely missing the point.
My path is my path.
My journey is my journey.
My destination is my destination.

But it isn't about the destination. It's about the journey.
It's about the current moment.
It's about the next step.
When I feel I can't continue, I need to stop and rest, look around me, admire the view, and take in the landscape.

As I sit here and ponder, I realise that the journey I have been on is <u>my</u> journey—no one else's. All the roads I have travelled have *served a purpose. The roads that have been most difficult and terrifying, threatening my very existence, have taught me the most. My experiences have contributed to me gaining an understanding that goes so much deeper than mere knowledge......*

I have learnt that when I'm at the bottom of a seemingly insurmountable mountain, I need to stop before mindlessly trying to scale its heights. Maybe I'm not meant to climb it. Just because others are already halfway up doesn't mean it's my mountain to climb. Maybe, I'm meant to just sit here and admire the view.
This mountain, the way it appears today, is unique to today. The way the light is hitting it, the clouds that are above it, the height of the grass that has grown on it, the flowers that are reflecting their own colour, the insects feeding off those plants, the animals that are using the trees and vegetation for food or shelter, the variety of birds and the songs they are singing – all of them are being captured by my senses in a unique combination that will never be exactly the same again. The light and clouds may be completely different tomorrow, creating another unique landscape. This mountain may have been here for millennia, viewed by generations of creatures and humans since time began. But today, it is my mountain.
How many people have just got on and scaled the mountain, missing out on their own unique encounter with this place that no other living being will have the opportunity to experience in the whole of eternity?

While sitting here, waiting for my next step to be revealed, I observe that many people are reaching the top of the mountain but cannot enjoy the view or take a moment to reflect on the path they have taken to get there; as soon as they reach the top they are looking for the next mountain to climb, looking for bigger and better challenges, never satisfied with what they have just achieved, driven to keep going. I realise that they are not actually moving forward towards their destiny. Instead, they are running away from their past......

I have learnt that, if my path takes me to the ocean, I don't have to always jump right in. Sometimes, I need to sit at the water's edge, breathe in the sea air, feel the sand between my toes and listen to the rhythmic sound of the waves as they lap against the shore. I have learnt that if I enter into the water, I don't always have to rigorously swim against the tide; sometimes, I need to tread water, and sometimes, I need to float on my back and let the heat of the sun shine down on me, sometimes I need to stop resisting and let the tide take me to where it wants to go, sometimes I need to scream out for a lifeboat to come and rescue me... and sometimes I just need to stop fighting it and let myself sink to the bottom of the ocean – I have been there enough times to know I won't drown, no matter how rough the waters or how long I am submerged for......

I have learnt that when my path is blocked by a raging fire, I don't always have to respond with blind panic and start screaming for help or frantically try to stamp it out. Sometimes, the fire doesn't need to be extinguished. Sometimes, I need to sit next to it without fear, find food to cook on it, warm my hands next to it, or be entranced as I watch the flames dance around until nothing is left except the glowing embers. Sometimes, I need to brace myself, dig deep and walk across the burning coals. Sometimes, the purpose of the fire is to purify me, so I need to stay in the heat of the moment until the dross separates out and rises to the surface, then evaporates into the atmosphere......

I have learnt to listen to my body when I am injured or in pain. There is a time to keep going, endure, overcome, and push through the pain. But there is also a time to stop, take in nourishment, let others clean and dress my wounds and give myself time to heal. If I don't discern the difference, I am likely to do myself much more *damage, which will take much longer to heal. I have also learnt that I do not need to cover up my scars and hide them in shame. My scars make me more beautiful. I should wear them as a badge of honour, a permanent reminder of the battles I have fought and won.........*

I have learnt that if I find myself in the midst of a raging storm, I do not instantly run for shelter when the lightning strikes. If I run in a blind panic to the wrong place, the very place that I thought would protect me could, in fact, put me in far greater danger. Sometimes, instead of praying to be sheltered from the storm, I should be praying for the courage and tenacity to stand firm and conquer my fears......

I have learnt that when I am on a long road with no end in sight, sometimes I need to walk, sometimes I need to run, sometimes I need to drive, and sometimes I need to hitch a lift. When I come to a crossroads, I need to take stock. My satnav always wants me to take the fastest route and get to the end as soon as possible, but maybe I'm not even meant to be going to the destination I thought I was heading to when I set off. Just because I am surrounded by people confidently speeding off, people who seem to know exactly where they are going and where their endpoint is, what route to take and which lane they need to be in to get there, I don't need to follow or try to keep up. They are the ones most likely to end up in the wrong place or in a serious collision......

The most important thing that I have learnt is that it is not about reaching the destination. It is all about the journey. It was never about the destination, and it was definitely never about getting to a better destination than others or getting there sooner. Ultimately, we will all end up at the same place. It was never intended to be a race or a competition. It was always, only ever, about the journey.

When we reach the end, we will all be shown a film, first of the route that was mapped out for us long before we got to the start line, and then of the journey we actually chose to take.
We will not be penalised for the times we ended up on the wrong path because of other people's actions, but we will be held accountable for the decisions that were ours to make.

Those of us who have tried to listen and done our best to stay true to the path set out for us, no matter how difficult or torturous, will be rewarded with a prize and a victor's crown. Most of all, we will be able to take a well-earned rest.

Those who missed the point, who did not follow their chosen path, who thought they knew best and didn't even stop to ask for advice, who were so obsessed about the destination that they took no notice of the route they were taking or the path they were on, who were in such a hurry they pushed others out the way and never stopped to help those who were stranded.....when they see how wrong they were, they will be so filled with regret, they will not be able to enter into eternal rest. They will end up begging to return, to be given another chance, in order to fulfill their true destiny………

MJA 24.10.23

The Journey

Standing on the threshold of a new dawn;
The journey to get here has taken so long.
There's no going back; I have to move on
My future is waiting, my past has gone......

As I stand on the brink of a life full of new promise
I feel anticipation but also fear.
Standing before me, the life I could only ever have dreamed of
Now, it's so close; it's already here!

But before I get ready to move on,
I need to stand here for a while,
Take time to reflect on just how far I have come,
The lessons learnt with every mile.

I look back on the road that has brought me to this place,
I see all the places I failed.
The dead ends, the roundabouts and all the wrong turns
The pits I fell into and the mountains I've scaled.

Many of my miles have been travelled alone,
Unnoticed, in the darkness of night;
No one can imagine the terrors I encountered,
Or how much I have had to fight.

I took a long detour through 'The Valley of Death',
Barely crawling along on my knees,
I only kept going because of the promise of still waters,
And dreams of soft, tender, green fields.

As I look back, I can see all the battlegrounds,
The fights I faced alone;
The wars in which I was totally overcome,
And the wars I fought and won.

I can see the people who travelled with me,
Walking the same road for a while,
I still feel the sadness as they went their separate ways,
When they realised my journey was so vile....

As I stand here reflecting on all that has passed
The landscape begins to unravel,
Before my eyes, many alternate paths,
Routes that I could have travelled.

As I watch, I notice the varied twists and turns,
With their myriads of possibilities
Every route revealing an alternate version of me,
And vastly different opportunities.

I am immediately filled with remorse and regret,
As I think about my history,
How different could this journey have been
If those things hadn't happened to me?

As I watch on, the scene begins to change:
Out of each and every path,
Numerous different versions of me
They are starting to emerge.

Like an army returning from a horrific war,
The fragmented parts of me,
Breaking out of their prisons of torture,
Finally, setting themselves free.

Many of them have visible scars,
Some still have open wounds,
All are slowly walking towards me,
Resolute and determined.

But as well as the children I knew were there,
Many more are marching forward.
All of the different versions of me
If I had taken a different road.

The "me" I would have been,
If I hadn't been abused,
The "me" I know I could have been,
If I had grown up feeling loved.

The versions of me that could have evolved,
If I had felt confident and secure
The "me" that would have had a completely different life,
If I hadn't been weighed down with manure.

The children I could have become mother to,
If the circumstances were different,
The "me" that could have lived with integrity,
If I hadn't been forced to pretend...

As each of these different versions of me
Come up to me in turn,
I am filled with love and deep gratitude,
And greet them with open arms.

As I welcome each and every one,
I hold them tight and don't let go.
As we remain transfixed in this embrace
They know they have finally come home.

I hold them close, and I start to feel whole,
As they dissolve into me;
For the first time ever, I know that I know,
That it's time for me to be free.

From this very moment, I can learn to fly,
I can be the real me,
The "me" I was first intended to be,
At the beginning of all eternity....

Now, I am ready to walk the new path,
That is opening in front of me.
I can dance, I can sing, I can celebrate my life.
I am completely free.

MJA 25.10.23

Chapter 21

"All change, please – we're heading to a new destination!"

I have asked myself so many times over the last 3 years, "Why?"

Why am I putting myself through the stress of revisiting that house of horrors over and over again? Of reliving the trauma and letting myself be overwhelmed with emotions that I can’t even put into words?

It's because I dream of a life where I can be my true, authentic self, where all of those children have been rescued and feel safe in the knowledge that they are worthy of love, affection, comfort, contentment, and security. A life where they have been fully accepted and reintegrated into a whole version of me. I dream of feeling at peace with my past, present and future rather than constantly running from my past, feeling overwhelmed in the present and fearing further mental health issues in the future.

I dreamed of this destination and started moving towards it back in 1991 when I started allowing myself to remember and sought support from others.

But that support was intermittent and often caused more harm than good. I have spent decades since that time having completely lost hope. Believing that I would never be able to disentangle myself from the toxic web woven by my family.

I have spent far more time stuck in the bottom of deep pits than I have moving forward. And yet something, deep inside my innate self, has not given up. Whenever I have seriously contemplated suicide, something has prevented me. Maybe, that "something" is that innate part of me that believes that at some point, I will make it to my dream destination!

The Pit – 2003

Once again, I find myself in the bottom of a deep pit.
Once again, it is cold and lonely and frightening.
Once again, I find myself angry and frustrated about being back in this place.
Oh, how I've told myself so many times that I'd never end up here again.
I'd try harder, be a better person, listen to all the advice and read all the self-help manuals I can find on how to steer clear of this trap.
But all the promises and positive thinking have failed me once again.
All that effort I put in, and where's it got me?

It wouldn't have been so bad, but I saw this one coming.
I read all the warning signs and saw it rapidly looming before me; I knew what was coming. I put all my energy into avoiding it at all costs.
But as soon as I got to the crucial moment, I fell right back in. Or maybe I jumped?

What did I do wrong? Why didn't I shout for help? Why didn't I stop myself?
I thought I wanted to stay out of my pit, but if I wanted to stay out of it that much, I would have avoided it. This is all my fault. I'm so pissed off with myself.
I'm sure I hate being in here, but is there some sort of sick part of me that enjoys it?
Is it my fault, or should somebody else have stopped me from falling?
Could I have stopped it, or has this pit got some sort of magnetic pull over me that is impossible for me to resist and overcome?

And then I realise... none of this matters. How or why I got here is irrelevant now.

The reality is that I'm here. Hungry, tired, disillusioned and alone.
I look up. I have fallen so far this time that I can't even see a shaft of light at the top.
I know that the outside world is up there somewhere.
I know that in the past I have struggled and struggled to climb back up.
But this time, it seems too far.
I almost always get hurt when I try to climb out.
Sometimes, I get halfway up and put all my energy and skills into clambering back up the steep slopes, only to lose my footing and slip back down, bruised and exhausted.
Anyway, what's the point in getting back to the top when every time I think I'm making some progress on my journey through the world, I end up back in the same place?
This time, I didn't have the energy to try again.
All I can do is sit, wishing things could be different....but they're not!

Total despair sets in.
In the depths of my despair, I hear distant voices.
Most people don't even realise I'm missing, but a few are starting to gather around the top.

The discussions begin......
"Not again! She was doing so well. I didn't realise she was anywhere near the pit!"
"It's an accident!"
"I bet she's done it on purpose! If you ask me, she enjoys being down there; otherwise, she wouldn't keep falling in!"
"Maybe she isn't even down there? Maybe she's just pretending and behaving as if she is there just to get attention?"
"I don't think there's anything wrong with her really".
"Why does she have to be so needy?"
"I think she's got an illness, so she can't avoid it!"
"Rubbish! Anyway, before we help her out, we need to make damn sure it won't happen again. Otherwise, we'll all be wasting our time!

After all, that's what she is, just a time waster. I don't think she really wants to come out; she must enjoy it down there. Otherwise, she wouldn't keep falling in."

As I listen, I go deeper into my despair.
Who do I believe? What am I meant to think? Does anyone understand? What does it matter anyway, now I'm here?
And then it dawns on me. I feel my stomach churn as I realise what's coming next.
I brace myself, and then it starts; the distant voices start to address me.....

"It's alright! I know why you're there! It's because of that thing that happened to you in your childhood. I know a good counsellor who can help you out!"
"It's not counselling she needs – I know a behaviour therapist! They will help her stop all this attention-seeking!"
"You don't need counselling or therapy; all you need is faith! Just stand on the Word of God and start telling yourself that you're not really down there, and you'll be back up in no time!"
I also hear the faint chanting as another group starts driving out all the evil spirits that are holding me down here.

I've heard it all before. Tried all the methods. Some of them work for a while, but I'm back down here, so none of them are truly effective.
What I really want is for someone to climb down, experience what I'm going through, then take me in their arms and lift me out. I want someone else to take responsibility for my situation because I can't.

But I know it won't happen.
In the past, I've tried to make it happen; I've started shouting and screaming and cutting myself up. I've tried starving myself and

letting myself get so near to death that surely, someone will have to come down and save me?
But all this has led to more labelling: "attention seeker", "personality disorder", "behavioural problem".
And still, no one comes to sit with me in the darkness.

Surely, if I manipulate some more, someone will prove their love for me by coming for me?
Perhaps, if the truth be known, I fall into this pit every time because I feel unloved and want somebody, somewhere, to prove how much they love me by getting me out.

But it won't happen. It never does.

Deep down, I know that this is my pit.
It is my journey.
No one else can pull me out.
I have to take responsibility to get myself out.
Yet I can't do it. I'm too disillusioned to try all their "methods" again, only for them not to work. I'm too exhausted to try and climb. What hope is there if it's down to me if no one else can do it for me, and yet I can't help myself?

Deeper despair sets in. I don't think I ever will get out this time....

But what is this?

In the silence, I am starting to hear a new voice.
I know I've never heard this one before.
As I listen, water floods over my soul like a soothing balm, for this voice is telling me something completely refreshing and totally new. It is telling me that it's OK to be where I am. Stop striving. Stop worrying. I don't have to do anything. Just wait. God is down here in this pit with me, just look for Him. Wait for His love to reach me. He doesn't blame me for falling. He's not even bothered if I don't

get back up again. All He wants is for me to let Him love me just where I am.
The other distant voices fade away.
I am left in the dark stillness.
Could it be that......?
I can hardly dare to believe that this could be true. All the time the "experts" have been judging and labelling me and advising me on how to get out of my pit, God Himself has been down here with me, silently watching and waiting...

In the deep darkness, a shaft of light penetrates the inside of my heart. How long has it been since I knew even the smallest ray of hope?

My lips silently start to move. Although nothing comes out of my mouth, my heart is shouting;
"God? Are you here? Could it be that You understand? Is it really possible that you don't blame me? Although you know I got it wrong again, are you not judging me like all the rest? Even here, in the depth of the darkness, You can see some good in my heart? That in the depths of my soul, You still love me?"

There is no earthquake or fire. I do not even hear a still, small voice in response.
Instead, I am overwhelmed with a sense of His presence as I am taken up in His arms and enveloped both internally and externally by His love.
There are no words to be said.
Everything in my heart is being poured out before Him without me saying a word.
For once, I can stop struggling, stop striving, and stop pretending that I'm capable of being someone I'm not.
I can simply "be" and experience the novelty of knowing I am truly accepted. That whatever I've done and whoever I am, that's good

enough. That I'm worthy of love, not because of what I have or haven't done, but simply because I am.

I am still in my pit. I have not been dramatically translated back to the top. Nor have the arms that surround me pulled me out.
But somehow, it doesn't matter anymore.
I really don't care if I stay here forever. It won't bother me if I never rejoin the normal people on their journeys along their straight roads.
Because in this darkest of all places, there is a new flame burning within me.
I am loved.
I am accepted.

I have discovered God in the depths.

MJA 2003

Chapter 22

"Shame on you!": The perpetuating cycles of toxic shame

The parts of me that still remain entrapped in the house of horrors have one thing in common; shame.

This is by far the most difficult emotion I have had to face – so difficult, in fact, that I haven't really faced up to it at all, which is why the parts that feel the most shame remain un-rescued.

A few weeks ago, I was thinking about the experiences that I intentionally left out of this book. All of them have one thing in common—when those memories flash through my mind, I am consumed with suffocating, intoxicating, overwhelming shame.

Apart from my counsellor, I have been unable to tell anyone about these experiences—partly because they are so extreme that I fear I will not be believed and partly because I am still too ashamed to admit they happened. For now, those experiences remain in that sacred space between counsellor and counselee.

The reason that this shame is so difficult to talk about is that I have never been able to find the words to express the feeling; it isn't just shame, but layer upon layer upon layer of shame that weighs me down and paralyses me; a sense that every fibre of my being is polluted and violated (see "HIV of the Soul on p. 69). Some people refer to it as "*toxic shame – an intense, long-lasting, debilitating feeling of unworthiness"* (https://psychcentral.com), but even those words do not even begin to describe it.

When I try to talk about it with my counsellor, I end up with my head down the toilet or going into "deep freeze."

Not only can I not put this emotion into words, but when I do feel it, I have no idea what I am meant to do with it. If I feel pain or rejection or abandonment, I can cry. If I feel threatened, I can shout at my counsellor to fuck off, run back into the grizzly cage and shut the door behind me; if I feel overwhelmed, I can curl up in a ball and go into freeze mode. But what am I meant to do with this?

Numerous books have been written about shame (see recommended reading list on p214.). I have at least six in my electronic library, all of which I gave up on in the first few chapters.

The reason? Everything I read on the topic says the same thing; that the way to resolve toxic shame is through learning *self-compassion*.

Those words never fail to throw me into a flying rage. They trigger a part of me who I haven't yet come to fully know or understand. What I do know is that when I hear the words *self-compassion*, I also hear patronising words being spoken to my fat, unlovable teenagers; "*God loves you the way you are*!" which I always interpreted as "*It's a good job God loves you, because no one else does*!"

So, when people tell me I need to learn self-compassion to heal my shame, what I'm really hearing is: "*You're going to have to learn to love yourself because no other bugger will!*"

My rational adult has already learnt that I am deeply, deeply loved and accepted by others. My healing adult can put a loving arm around some of the parts that have been rescued, and is learning to nurture and care for my body tenderly. But whatever words you might want to use to describe this, I cannot and will not ever call it self-compassion!

When it comes to shame, I feel stuck in a perpetual cycle;

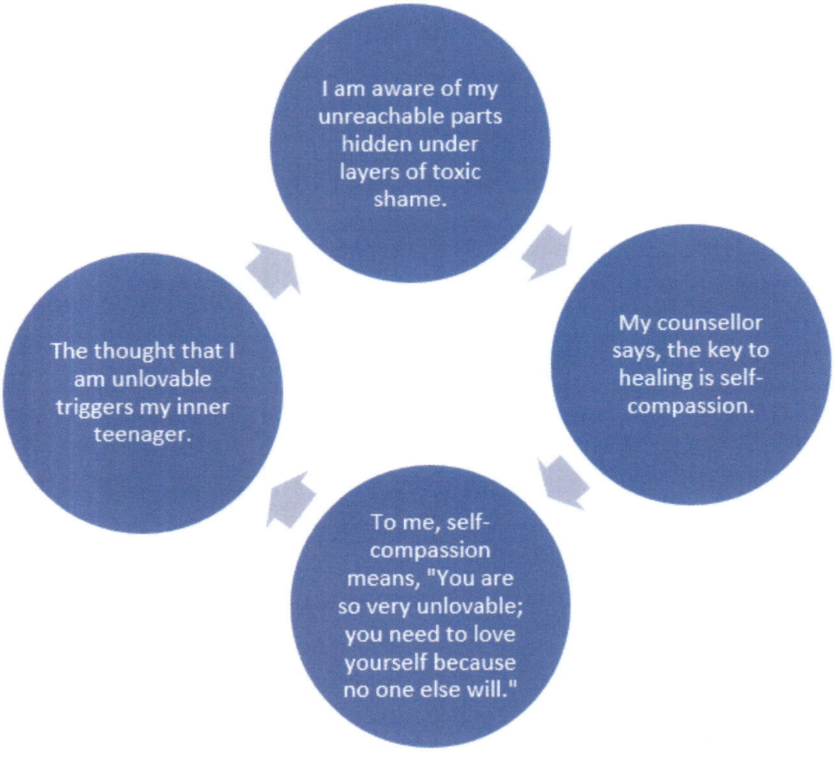

The Pit – 2022

I'm back in the bottom of the pit.
Although I've been in a similar place so many times before, this time feels completely different.
It's the first time I've ended up here in over 10 years. During that time, I've actually found myself walking along a scenic path, getting a taste of what it's like to get some pleasure along the way, actually enjoying the journey rather than fighting and struggling for every step.
Along this road, I've also found some very faithful companions. I've learnt what it's like to have someone to look out for me, hold out a hand to help me over the more difficult terrain and enjoy the nice moments with me.

But here I am, back in the depths again. It feels dark and lonely like it did before.
Although some things feel the same, in other ways, it feels very unfamiliar.
One thing that is very different is that there are no distant voices at the top chuntering, labelling or judging me. There seems to have been quite a big change in people's attitudes over the last 20 years – or maybe it's just that I'm on the road with very different people around me? Either way, the people on this route seem to understand that it's not unusual for people to find themselves in a pit. They also seem to understand that when someone is down a pit, they can't just be dragged out or helped to pull themselves out by quick-fix solutions. Sometimes, people just need someone to sit with them in the darkness.

Something else is very different this time. While I've been sitting down here, I've been watching a slide show from my past—it's like a cine film being projected onto the pit walls in an almost continuous loop. It keeps showing images from a horror movie, with such unimaginable scenes of terror that there are no words to describe them. Sometimes, the images come with sounds and smells, but most of the time, they are just disjointed clips that have been badly edited together.

The trouble is, I can't make sense of most of it. Most of the time, I have to tell myself this has to be made up, that nothing this horrific could have taken place in reality, that this is all just a result of an overly vivid imagination. I try and turn the movie off when I can. I have learnt lots of ways of distracting myself with other things – although it's often near impossible to find effective ways of doing this when you're in a deep hole. It takes a lot of effort, and as soon as I get tired or try to go off to sleep it's starts over again.

My new companions can't see the film for themselves, so they are relying on me to describe it too them. The trouble is I often just can't find the words. When I do manage to give them a sketchy outline, they can get quite emotional about the things that were done to me in the film. They get angry and upset and want to get some kind of justice for what the other actors in the storyline did to me. This makes me feel quite uncomfortable as most of the time, I watch on without any emotion. I feel like I should be feeling something, but most of the time, I'm not.

What's made things worse is that more recently, the cine film has been showing a new storyline with a different actor, which is even more unbelievable than the original production. Every time I see it, I am traumatised; I feel sick and have intense knots in my stomach. I try to switch it off, but I can't.
I've only been able to tell one person about this new storyline. I keep telling them I must have made it all up, and it's all some elaborate fantasy, but they don't think so. When I think about it rationally, this new sub-plot fills in quite a few gaps that had been left unexplained by the original film – it answers many unanswered questions. My companions reassure me that it's no wonder I've

fallen into the pit so many times on my journey, that none of it is my fault, that it's a miracle I've survived, especially when I've been negotiating the treacherous paths on my own for so long......

But here's the thing. My interpretation of this new storyline is different to theirs. I feel that what happened to me in these new scenes is my fault. I was old enough to stop it. I could have chosen to change the storyline to a different one, but I chose not to. I somehow deserve the punishment, humiliation and degradation. It doesn't matter how much my companions tell me that this isn't the case, it doesn't change how I feel. Every time the movie replays, I feel like I'm drowning in layers and layers of shame. This is what makes this pit so very different to the ones I've been in before.
As I sit here, I feel like I'm swimming in an ocean of shit and that I've absorbed so much of it I'm polluted on the inside as well as plastered with it on the outside.
I've tried so hard to stop paddling, to be still, and to reconnect with that still, small voice I found at the bottom of my last pit. I've tried to imagine that shaft of light penetrating through the layers of sewage. But it's just not happening. And at the moment, I'm not even sure it ever will. This pit seems darker than any that have gone before; it feels completely different.
I'm not sure what I'm meant to be doing while I'm down here – all the methods I've used in the past to survive just aren't working this time. Distraction techniques take a whole lot of energy that I don't always have, and even when I manage to use them effectively, they don't do anything to help me climb back up towards the light. I feel so stuck and frustrated. I feel like I owe it to my companions to get back out on the road and journey with them again, but I can't, and at the moment, I'm not sure I ever will.

MJA 11.3.22

Chapter 23

The endless cycles of grief

Coming out of a place of denial and facing your trauma head-on is likely to trigger very strong grief, anger and deep despair. You cannot do this part of the journey alone. It is hard, painful and exhausting.

During my nursing training, I was introduced to Kubler Ross's work on "The Stages of Grief" (Kubler-Ross 1969). This gave me the impression that grief was a pretty straightforward process. Over time, you would move through the stages (denial, anger, bargaining, depression, acceptance) in a predictable, straightforward manner until you eventually "came out" on the other side!

Most people will tell you that this absolutely isn't the case, and that grief is a messy process. Just as you think you are getting somewhere, something unexpected happens; you get knocked off your feet and instantly feel like you are back where you started!

After almost three years on this journey, I think I can finally say I have got through the denial. This, in itself, is a miracle, given all that my family did to convince me I was making it up. Every now and then, when I am releasing deep emotion in relation to a specific memory, I feel the need to ask my counsellor, *"Are you absolutely sure I haven't made this up?"* But this is more out of a need for reassurance and validity of my emotions rather than me really questioning my reality.

When I am going through this deep catharsis, once I have released the initial pain, I move into the bargaining phase: "*Why wasn't anyone there?,*" "*Why didn't anyone see what he was doing to me?*" "*Why didn't anyone care enough to stop him?*" "*Why couldn't God have let him die when I was three, so it didn't keep happening?*" And when my counsellor quietly whispers, "*I don't know*", I am hit with an even more powerful wave of isolation, desolation, abandonment and alone-ness. In the days following these cathartic sessions, I usually experience deep, deep sadness. For the first two years, this would manifest itself in hopelessness and despair. I would often express suicidal ideation. Although I knew deep down I didn't want to die, I did not know how to live with the feelings. Now, more often than not, the sadness makes me want to hold which ever part of me has been surfacing and tell them they are no longer alone.

So far, I have not experienced anger. In the beginning, I would often scream at my counsellor to fuck off, but that wasn't real anger; it was the "kitten behind the boiler syndrome". I often go into sessions feeling like I just want to shout and scream at her (not that I have any reason to), but it never actually happens.

Whenever she has tried to bring up the subject of anger, more often than not, I will reply, "I don't get angry " and if she pushes me any further, I go into "deep freeze".

In recent weeks, I have been able to talk about the hatred I have towards my father. I hated him with pure hatred from the age of 3. I tried not to, but it was always there, bubbling beneath the surface. In all the years I was trying to be a Christian, I had to pretend it wasn't there, as I always had it drummed into me that Christians couldn't hate people. They had to forgive them instead. I spent years getting up every morning, praying and praying to forgive him, but the feelings never went away, so in the end, I decided I couldn't be a Christian.

But hatred is different to anger. And, up to now, I have never felt any anger towards him or my mum. In recent weeks, I have found myself shouting and screaming at him in my head as I am trying to go to sleep, and I hear my silent screams echoing through my head, wishing I could find a way to let them out. But as yet, it hasn’t happened.

From the age of three, I would pray that God would let my father die so that I could have the relationship with my mum that I craved. Instead, he lived to the age of 87 and by the time he died, my mum was in the very advanced stages of dementia. I felt nothing but relief when he died. The outpouring of emotion I expressed at his funeral was not the pain of loss but an explosion of indescribable feelings that were now safe to release after over 50 years of containment. Five years on, I have not once thought of him without feeling relief that he has gone. There is not a single thing about him that I miss. Just the thought of him still causes a foul, burning stench in the back of my nose and an acidic, nauseating taste in my mouth, and I feel an indescribable sense of repulsion and disgust - now directed towards him rather than myself, but still as strong as ever.

When friends lose a parent and are grieving, I feel I have nothing to say and don't know how to respond to them, as I cannot begin to imagine what it would feel like to experience anything but relief for the loss of a parent.

But the *most* difficult aspect of grief that I still continually face is not in relation to my father. Instead, it is due to the lack of attention from my mum, which I always deeply yearned for. As described on p61, when I stopped my addictive behaviours (which were all aimed at manipulating love and attention from women), I went into avoidance and denial. The indescribable pain that rips through the core of my being when I allow myself to recognise that deep longing is too unbearable.

The Depths of My Heart

This artwork symbolises the emptiness, abandonment, desolation, and aloneness of never, ever feeling love, acceptance, nurture, and protection from my Mum. It feels like an eternal, fathomless, bottomless vacuum, like a black hole in space.

As soon as I let myself consider the possibility of opening myself up to love and compassion from another woman, it exposes my brokenness. It has been far, far easier in the last 15 years to tell myself I can live without it and that I just have to accept that I will never find healing because the wound is too great. I have managed to keep all my relationships with women distant and detached for so long now.

Admitting that I want/need that love and compassion and allowing myself to get a taste of it is not soothing. It is like ripping the scab off to expose the unhealed wound; it is painful and hurts more than I can put into words. I am frightened to let myself admit the need because as soon as I get just a small drop of acceptance, it reminds me of how unquenchable my thirst for a woman's love is. I feel vulnerable. I feel exposed. I feel more pain and heartache than I can describe in words. And more than anything else, I'm frightened. Frightened that I am so, so needy, history will repeat itself; whenever I have allowed myself to need another woman's love, it has always ended in them walking away before I have had the chance to heal because I have been "too needy" and asked for more than they have been able to give.

MJA 9.6.22
©AIMtogetbetter2024

For over 15 years, my husband tried to get me to break links with my family. But I kept going to visit my mum every few days. I always came back upset and disappointed. I always went with the hope that this time, it would be different and that I would get what I had always desperately longed for from her. But I never did.

During the early years of her journey with dementia, I experienced deep despair, realising that, even if my father did die, it was too late for me to ever have the relationship with her that I longed for. After my father died, I continued to visit her two to three times a week. I didn't understand why I was so driven to keep going; even when her dementia was at such an advanced stage, she did not say a single word, and there was never any recognition or response from her.

It wasn't out of a sense of duty—I knew I didn't owe her anything. Very recently, I have had to admit to myself that, although in my head I knew it was never going to happen, I kept going back because, in my heart, I was desperately longing to get something from her that she had never been able to give—genuine love.

When she died, I was surprised with how overwhelmed with grief I was. But I knew I wasn't grieving a loss. I was grieving for what I never had.

Letting go

How can I be grieving so much
For something I never had.
How is it possible to feel so much pain
For losing such a toxic love?

Why is it so hard to let go
Of something I could never grasp?
Why am I so reluctant to close the door
On such a traumatic past?

Why is it so difficult to walk away
When all you did was hurt me?
Why do I keep myself bound by your chains
When I long to be set free?

I knew that your acceptance of me
Was reliant on me playing the game;
If I refused to play "happy families",
You'd reject me again and again.

Your love of me was conditional
On me hiding behind your masks;
You would only let me feel I belonged
If I lived up to your false image.

Why, when I remember all those years of abuse
Do I drown in a sea of shame?
Why do I insist on punishing myself
And continue to take all the blame?

Why do I feel so much guilt
When I didn't do anything wrong?
Why, when I knew your love would only hurt me,
Was my need of you so strong?

How can I feel such longing?
For a love I never knew.
Why is it so difficult to say goodbye
To the person that wasn't you?

Now, I have to let go of that lifelong desire
To feel loved and accepted by you;
The hope that things could be different has gone,
Those dreams have died with you.

Why am I feeling so much despair
To say goodbye for the very last time?
Letting go of what was never there,
Losing something that was never mine.

MJA 28.3.22

In the last few weeks, I have returned to this place of grief. Up to now, I have spent very few of my counselling sessions talking about my feelings about my mum because I am so frightened by the pain and what lies behind it.

But this time around, it feels slightly different. Instead of going into a frenzy of fear I am just sitting with the feelings. Instead of avoiding them through behaviours or filling the emptiness with food, alcohol, or activity, I am just allowing whatever needs to happen to happen.

It is by far the most difficult thing I have had to do yet. Although I feel a physical pain piercing through my heart and searing through my very depths, it is too deep for me to express through tears.

As I feel my heart shatter into pieces, it leaves vast nothingness. A deep vacuum of emptiness.

If I imagine standing in front of my father, I am still overwhelmed with negative emotions, but if I imagine standing in front of my mum, there is absolutely nothing. No positive emotion, no negative. Just an eternal black hole. At this moment in time, I have absolutely no idea if it will ever change.

So why do I keep persevering with this journey if, when I am not stuck in a pit, I am going around in circles?

Recently, I realised that every time it *seems* as if I am coming back to the same place, if I stay still for long enough, I notice that something is different from the last time I was here. Sometimes, I realise that I have changed, and at others, I realise that my perspective of this landscape is different, and I view it in a slightly different way. Sometimes, these changes are so imperceptibly small I don't see them, and I need my counsellor to point them out to me.

This is what gives me hope that one day, I will be able to move on and leave this place behind me for good.

I have learnt that in moments of deepest pain, despair, or abandonment, I need to still myself and listen out for the Song of the Butterfly. It is these songs of hope that remind me of my destination and give me the strength and determination to keep moving forward.

PART V

Songs of the Butterfly

Chapter 24

What Is It About Butterflies?

Yesterday, we visited a butterfly farm.
I have always loved butterflies, but they have become far more significant to me in the last few years. As we walked through the butterfly enclosure, I was captivated by butterflies of all sizes and colours flew around our heads, sat on plants and leaves or came to settle on people. The part I was most mesmerised with was the hatching area, where we could actually watch new butterflies emerge out of the hanging chrysalises.
It wasn't just me – children and adults alike were taking great delight and interest in these beautiful, delicate creatures.

What is it about butterflies that seem to captivate us?

- Butterflies are a sign of hope. I've been told that after the Holocaust they discovered many butterflies carved into the walls of the cells by the Jewish prisoners of war as they awaited their fate in the gas chambers.
- Butterflies are a sign of the summer; the season of light, sunshine, warmth and colour.
- Butterflies have such simple grace and beauty. They do not see their own wings, they just get on with being themselves without ego, without self-consciousness, without trying to change their appearance or the colour or pattern of their wings to please others, they just fly, doing their own thing, having no idea that others get such delight from the beauty they radiate.
- Butterflies can take off and fly whenever danger comes close, rising high above whatever is attempting to threaten them.
- Butterflies are also very vulnerable; in the wrong hands it would take nothing for them to be crushed and destroyed. As with many other things in our natural world, the thing that

makes them so beautiful and attractive to humans is their simple, graceful, delicacy and vulnerability. The very characteristics that attract some in a positive way, also attracts predators. Millions of butterflies have been lured into traps and nets, taken into captivity, killed, pinned down and put on display in museums or wall mountings. The humans who do this, and have done so for centuries, justify their behaviour saying it is their interest, love and fascination of the creature that motivates them to do this. But how can anyone who captures, pins down and destroys such a delicate, vulnerable, defenceless creature think that they are motivated by love?

- *Perhaps the most fascinating thing about butterflies is that they're not born as butterflies. They start out as ugly, slimy caterpillars. At some point the caterpillar has to stop being a caterpillar. It has to find a safe place, spin itself a cocoon to protect itself, then let its outer layers of skin dissolve. In the darkness, it turns into a gooey mess, that somehow, over time, metamorphosises into a beautiful butterfly. When it eventually emerges, it is still not ready to fly. It needs time to hang for a while to give its wings time to dry and get used to the new environment outside of the chrysalis. But eventually, when it's good and ready, it just spreads its wings and flies.*
- *Depending on the type of butterfly, the process of going from an egg to a caterpillar to chrysalis to a butterfly can take as long, if not much longer than the time it has spent living as a butterfly, but the wait is worth it. It has fulfilled its destiny.*

How many humans never fulfil their true destiny or potential because they don't realise that they are not meant to stay as a caterpillar forever? Or because they are too safe in their identity as a caterpillar to be willing to change? Or because they fear the process of metamorphosis, knowing it will be a dark, lonely, messy, uncomfortable process? They long to be that butterfly, but the journey to get there is too daunting, too frightening, too painful, too difficult to face.

MJA 14.6.24

If she wasn't completely unlovable, why did she feel so unloved?

If she wasn't completely unlovable
Why did she feel so unloved?
If she wasn't totally unreachable
Why was she so alone?

If she wasn't completely unacceptable
Why did she feel she was "made wrong?"
If her life wasn't totally untenable
Why did she never feel she belonged?

If her life was meant to have purpose
Why did she feel like such a big mistake?
Why was her body so detestable;
A lump of meat for others to rape?

If those children weren't made completely of shit
Why does the thought of them make me want to vomit?
If they are more than just a biproduct of his fithy lust
Why does their existence consume me with disgust?

Why, if she wasn't making it all up,
Were her stories never believed?
If he really was that monster (not a good Christian man),
How could everyone be so deceived?

Why, oh why, if it wasn't her fault
Has she always had to carry the blame?
Why, if she wasn't meant to carry the guilt
Is she buried deep under layers of shame?

Spirit's reply:

Come, my child, be still for a while
Let me try to explain why
Everything they taught you about love
Was, in fact, a lie.

Everything that you thought was love
Was, actually, abuse;
People using you for their own selfish desire
Defiling you, mocking you, then making you out to be the liar.

Everything they taught you about "God" was fake,
Using religion to promote their own image;
Blaming you for all their mistakes,
Drowning you in guilt, instead of adorning you with my grace.

Their acceptance of you was based on a lie,
On you always having to perform;
Being careful not to give the secret away,
Getting punished when you wouldn't conform.

But the greatest injustice, the thing that makes me so sad,
Is that they told you that you were mad;
They made you think that I made you wrong,
They stripped away your identity, extinguished your unique song.

So, now, let me tell you what true love is like,
It's time to expose all the lies,
I want to change the way you think about your past
So you can move on with the rest of your life...

My love is out in the open,
It is a pure, cleansing bright light,
It doesn't have to be kept a secret,
Or be hidden in the darkness of night.

My love is pure and unlimited,
It is not proud or arrogant or rude,
It is not based on you meeting conditions
Or following a set of rules.

My love is patient, my love is kind,
It doesn't stop when you do something wrong,
My love is never self-seeking,
It doesn't demand anything in return.

My love will never hurt you,
It will never cause you pain,
My love will always cleanse you,
It will never make you feel shame.

My love will always believe in you,
Fill you with faith, not with self-doubt,
My love sees your potential in everything,
It will always give you hope.

My heart overflows with compassion
You are so beautiful in my eyes
You are my spectacular creation
You are my pure, unblemished bride...

And so, my love, are you beginning to see
That for your whole life you've been deceived?
Everything they taught you and made you believe
Was all about them, and not about Me.

And now, my love, I want this truth to burn through you
Like a purifying flame;
None of this was your fault...
You were not to blame.

MJA 12.6.22

This Girl

What do you see when you look at me?
Do you want to judge and criticise?
Do you secretly wonder why I'm so "messed up"
Without daring to look into my eyes?

What do you see when you look at me?
Would it come as a complete surprise
To discover that what you think is me
Is in fact, an elaborate disguise?

I've hidden behind it, projected a false image
To prevent anyone getting too close
Because behind those defences and impenetrable walls
Lie dark secrets of inescapable abuse.

The disguise was so effective, it seemed so real,
It enabled me to escape my reality;
Even I was convinced that this unreachable soul
Was my true identity.

But now someone has come to rescue me,
Fought their way through the impenetrable walls;
They have shown me that this repulsive, disgusting, piece of shit
Isn't me at all.

They have slowly helped me to take off my disguise,
To escape the prison of my past,
So now it's time to expose all the lies
And introduce you to the real me, at last...

This girl is extremely courageous,
Despite a lifetime of pain,
She audaciously confronts all her demons
And boldly overthrows their shame.

This girl is strong and victorious,
Winning daily unseen wars,
Her silent screams are her battle cry
As she fights for an unrecognised cause.

This girl is brave and magnificent,
Beauty radiates from her scars,
Her wounds are her medals of glory,
Made stronger by embracing her fears

This girl is stubbornly tenacious,
Hanging on to life by a thread,
Determinedly clinging on to existence,
When really she should be dead.

This girl is noble and dignified,
Worthy of honour and respect,
Poised with honesty and integrity;
'What you see is what you get.'

This girl is graceful and elegant,
Caring and outrageously kind,
She is interesting and deeply curious
and listens with an open mind.

This girl is incredibly spectacular,
Majestic and sublime;
Dig deep and you will find hidden treasures
- A truly remarkable find...

But this girl is no one special;
Open your eyes and you will see
That you are completely surrounded,
By girls just as magnificent as me

MJA 23.6.23

Sing Your Song Part 1

Everyone who ever existed was created in order to compose and play a unique song, each with its own set of notes and chords. The individual notes, chords, bars and lines may seem meaningless when played on their own, but when they come together, every single composition, with its own unique combination of sounds, makes a recognisable song that touches My heart and brings Me so much pleasure.

Some songs are clearly recognisable from the first few bars being played.

Others have to be listened to for some time before it becomes clear what the tune is.

Some songs become known around the whole world. Some are remembered and replayed for hundreds of years after their completion.

Some people listen to other people's songs, and because they seem so popular and loved by so many, they try to copy them. This makes Me so sad, because they spend their whole lives playing out someone else's song, rather than letting their own tune be heard. They get to the end of their lives without ever discovering the unique song I wanted them to play.

Some songs, the ones that seem to be most popular, are written in a major key. People like listening to them because the song lifts their spirits.

But some of the most beautiful songs that have ever been written are in the minor key. They are often the ones that have been written and sung in secret; the ones that the general population have never even heard; sung in private but never shared, because the singer doesn't think others will want to listen. Those songs are often the most genuine, sung from the heart, with humility. They often tell a story of brokenness or heartache or pain. They may not be as popular to the masses because listening to them may make people sad. But to Me, they are beautiful because they are genuine. They touch my heart, and I love listening to them.

Many of these songs, played in the minor keys, contain discords. Some people hate listening to songs containing discords because it makes them feel uncomfortable. It is true, that in the moment the discord is being played, the listeners know that something isn't right, and it isn't comfortable to listen to. But anyone who knows anything about music understands that there is a very special moment, just after the discord is played and allowed to ring through the air, a "pregnant pause", sometimes long, sometimes inconceivably short, but a moment of silence, and of anticipation, a moment of waiting... because what comes next, whether it's in the next note or the next bar or the next line... is a resolution to the discord.
Some people will refuse to listen to such discordant music – they just hear an unpleasant noise; they may get up and try to turn the music off or walk away because they just don't understand.
But there are many, especially those who have studied music, for whom those discordant pieces are the most beautiful. They understand that there is something almost magical about these compositions. They are happy to sit through the discord, knowing that the reason discords are included in compositions is because in almost all cases, the discord gets resolved, creating a sense of satisfaction that is never experienced when listening to songs that do not have any discords. Any pieces of music that end without this resolution feel "unfinished". But those that do get resolved seem far more beautiful and satisfying to listen to than those more popular pieces, written in the major key.

And now, My love, let us talk about your unique song...

I know you are really struggling to keep your song playing.
There are so many lines that you would rather not be there.
But you only feel that way because much of your song has been written in the minor key and contains so many discords that people around you did not want to listen.
You need to understand that those people have many discords in their own song, but instead of letting them be resolved, they don't

own it – they are going through life trying to play someone else's song, rather than embracing their own.
There is no way they can listen to the discords in your song while they are pretending that there aren't any in theirs. They have worked for years to rub out the bars and lines in your song that they don't want to listen to, convincing you that they were never there...

I have had to take you on a journey, to rediscover those missing lines. I know it has been extremely uncomfortable. There are lots of bars in your song that are so discordant, at the moment, it sounds like a lot of loud, clanging, unpleasant sounds ringing through your ears. As you are rediscovering them, they are replaying over and over in your head. You are so overwhelmed with the noise that you have considered trying to stop the song playing for good...
But if you did that, your song wouldn't just be deleted, as if it never existed; it will remain unfinished for eternity, because no one else can finish your song for you.

You have spent much time wishing you could find a way of non-existing, of decomposing all the notes and chords of your song, of going back so none of it was ever written in the first place... but you know that is impossible.

Please, please don't end your song here, because the most beautiful bit is yet to come.

I had to take you back to rediscover those missing bits that others tried forcing you to delete. And I understand there are some bars in your song that are almost unbearable to listen to.
I also know that, at the moment, all you can hear is noise. You have been trying to push away those people who have been wanting to share your song, because you are ashamed of all the tangled discordant notes that you think have ruined your composition. You think people won't want to hear those lines...

Please, just take a step back and look...

Those bars that you would rather weren't there aren't all that your song contains...
Look, and you will see that between those bars, there have been notes that have brought so much pleasure to my heart, and to those around you...

Now, take a closer look at the music. Look at the whole piece of music from where you are now.
Yes, there are many, many bars of very discordant, unpleasant noise. But after each of those bars, there is a gap. That's because the process of recovering those lost parts of your song isn't yet complete...

I promise you, that for every single discord in your song, I am going to bring a resolution. Only then, will the process of restoration be complete. It has taken a long time for you to uncover all those lines that people persuaded you to rub out. Now, we have to go back to each one. I need you to spend time letting each discordant note be played, giving it the time and space to ring out through the universe. You will need to sit in that space, waiting, pausing, anticipating. I promise you, that if you do that, the resolution will come. Out of the discord and chaotic noise will come a harmony that you can't even imagine possible.

So please, please don't try to end your song now, because it isn't yet finished. I am longing for the day when those missing bars are filled in. I am in the process of creating a beautiful masterpiece. Once it is complete, those unpleasant discordant bars will still be there, but to every discord there will be a beautiful resolution, making the whole composition so much more beautiful and interesting to listen to...

Embrace your unique song and sing it.
Please, don't try to delete it.
I want your completed, beautiful composition to be played for all of eternity.
If you don't let that happen, there will be a gap in my collection forever, that no one else's song will be able to fill...

MJA 7.9.22

Sing your song

Sing your song
My beautiful one,
Like a bird announcing a new dawn;
I long to hear the sound of the notes
That have played since the day you were born.

Sing your song
My beloved one,
It's like music to my ears;
I want to listen to the unique sound
That you've created over the years.

Sing your song
My lovely one,
I long to hear your words.
Don't try to play someone else's tune;
I need <u>your</u> story to be heard.

Sing it from the mountain tops,
Sing it from the depths of the sea,
Sing it from the battle ground,
Sing it in times of peace.

Sing it with choirs of angels
So it resounds across eternity;
Sing it when you're all alone,
When the only one who hears it is me.

Sing your song in the morning
When the sunrise brings hope and new light,
Keep singing when the vacuum of despair
Sucks you into the darkest night.

Sing it with a beautiful descant
When you're flying like a butterfly,
Sing it with a booming base
When thunderclouds fill your sky.

Sing your song gently,
Like the breeze through the rustling leaves;
Let it bellow out loudly
When navigating stormy seas.

Sing your song as a melody,
When you have a story to tell;
I want to hear your sweet harmonies
When everything is going well.

Sing your song in the silence
When you're too scared to make a noise,
I'll hear the rhythm of your beating, broken heart
When fear has stolen your voice.

I know you've wanted to cut your song short
When you don't like the sound of the notes,
But the sound of those discords getting resolved
Are the parts I love the most.

So, sing when it sounds like a terrible noise,
When it feels like it's all gone wrong;
Those out of tune, tumultuous sounds
<u>Must</u> be included in your song.

So, sing your song to the very end
It's a masterpiece of beauty,
Every note tells of who you've become
In all your damaged glory.

Yours is a song no one else can sing,
So, sing it out, and set yourself free;
There will never be another voice like yours
In the whole of eternity.

MJA 8.10.22

The Echoes of the Universe

Every one of your silent screams
That echoed across the expanse of time;
All of them will now return to you
In the sound of a beautiful song.

Every time you let out your inaudible cries
They resounded through eternity,
And now come back, in the form of healing waves
Crashing on the shore of the sea.

Each of those invisible tears
That fell, unnoticed, down your cheeks,
Were secretly bottled over the years
And now reappear, as dewdrops on Autumn leaves.

Your broken heart, your shattered dreams,
Every unheard desire to die,
Will be replaced by the promise of hope and new life
When you see a rainbow scanning the sky.

For every moment your longing for love went unheard
And you felt the emptiness of unmet needs,
Mother Nature will wrap you in her arms of love,
Whisper words of acceptance in the gentle breeze.

Man has tried his best to desecrate and destroy
In order to feel more power,
But he will <u>never</u> be able to overcome
The delicate beauty in every flower.

He doesn't care what damage he does
To look good in others' eyes
But he will never be able to compete
With the grandeur of a crimson sunrise.

There is so much beauty surrounding you
That has grown out of a place of deep pain.
Like the stars, you will radiate glory
Because you once absorbed such shame.

So, stop. Breathe. Wait patiently for the rebound.
Listen in silence until you hear the words:
"Your healing is here – it has been found
In the echoes of the universe."

MJA 24.7.24

Epilogue

This book is for the bulls and the bears who may not yet have realised that this is not all there is and that this is not who they were destined to be.

This book is also for the caterpillars, who know they were always destined to be a butterfly but are too invested in their identity as a caterpillar to risk changing, or too scared of going through the process of metamorphosis, which is an essential stage that any caterpillar has to go through in order to find their true destiny.

It is also for those currently in the chrysalis; that dark, lonely and often very scary place, where the painful process of shedding those defensive outer layers and exposing what lies beneath is taking place. Especially those who are losing hope, getting impatient, wondering why it is taking so long, or asking if all this pain is really worth it. Hang on in there, it really will be worth the wait!

This book is for the butterflies, newly emerging from the chrysalis, who need time to dry their wings before they can fly.

And for the butterflies with broken wings. Be patient; it is nearly your time.

And for those butterflies who are already completely free, flying high and fulfilling their destiny; look out for me - I will be joining you shortly!

If you are a professional or an informal carer trying to support the bulls, the bears and the caterpillars, or holding a chrysalis in a warm, safe place, patiently waiting for, and willing the butterfly to emerge, I hope the things in this book can help you in your endeavours, and give you the patience and understanding you need as you wait

MJ Albutt, October 2024

References and Recommended Reading

Brown, B. (2012). "*Daring Greatly: How the Courage to Be Vulnerable Transforms the Way We Live, Love, Parent, and Lead*"". New York, Gotham Books.

Kubler-Ross, E. (1969). "*On death and dying*". The MacMillan company. New York.

Holland, T. (2024). "*The Imposter Syndrome Gremlin*". Presentation given at PGR conference, Worcester University 24.6.24.

Molnar, G. (2024). "*Imposter Syndrome*". Presentation given at PGR conference, Worcester University 24.6.24.

Mate, G. (2022). "*The one you feed*". Podcast 16.9.2022. Available from: www.alcoholfree.com

O'Donohue, J. (2003). "*Divine Beauty: The Invisible Embrace*". Bantam Books.

Rohr, R. (2003). "*True self, False self*". Franciscan Media.

Recommended Reading:

Engel, B'. (2014). "*It wasn't your fault: freeing yourself from the shame of childhood abuse with the power of self-compassion*". Brilliance Audio.

McDaniel, K. (2021). "*Mother Hunger*". Hay House, Inc.

McLaren, B. (2021). "*Faith after doubt*". Hodder and Stoughton.

Perry, B. & Winfrey, O. (2021). "*What happened to you? Conversations on trauma, resilience and healing*". Bluebird Books for Life.

Spring, C. (2019). "*Unshame*". Carolyn Spring Publishing. MediaCityUK. Salford.

Paperback available at: www.carolinespring.com/unshame-book

Available on Kindle at: https://amzn.to/2Wnj6Fu

Van der Kolk, V. (2029). "*The Body Keeps the Score*". Penguin.

Printed in Great Britain
by Amazon

62288531-10fc-409d-b994-2f6eb4739409R01